MAKE BOLD THINGS HAPPEN

Praise for *MAKE BOLD THINGS HAPPEN*

"Steve has always been a can-do first person. He is one of the first to offer to help regardless of who you are, or where you stand in life."

— Mark Segal, Publisher of *Philadelphia Gay News*
and author of *And Then I Danced*

"I've had the benefit of a front-row seat as Steve continually reinvents himself. His successes speak for themselves, and his book provides valuable insights that can help anyone achieve their personal and professional goals."

—Joe Zeff, President, Joe Zeff Design, Inc.

"Steve is a doer. When people struggle with how to start, he always begins with action. Steve believes that success begins with taking immediate action and that progress is grounded in doing. He motivates and build confidence with teams to keep moving forward by getting things done."

— Angela Val, President & CEO, Visit Philadelphia

"When things get complicated and off track, as they will, Steve is a guy that sees through the clutter, and with a sense of urgency clears the obstacles and inserts a plan."

—Alan Jacobson, CEO, J2 / Exit

"Steve is one of those extraordinary individuals who gets it. And gets it done!"

—Paul Silberberg, Chairman, Concierge Insurance Solutions
and author of *The Ethical Entrepreneur*

"Steve is one of the best people I've worked with in a 40+ year career. When I needed help with major projects, Steve was my first call. He is smart, talented, has a great sense of humor, doesn't take himself too seriously, and always gets results. Steve has a tremendous ability to cut through what is not relevant and hone in on what's important. He's value added to any project."

—Jim Cuorato, President and CEO,
Independence Visitor Center Corporation

"Steve's no-nonsense approach to life and his professional career has been an inspiration throughout the 15+ years I have known him. He brings passion and dedication to his work and to getting the job done. It has been a pleasure to watch him advocate for countless community groups and stand up for what he believes is right. He cares deeply for his friends and colleagues and will do anything for them when in need. I owe him a debt of gratitude for giving me my start in hospitality and am proud to call him a true friend and colleague."

— Kelley Maddox, VP of Sales, Live! Casino & Hotel Philadelphia

MAKE BOLD THINGS HAPPEN

INSPIRATIONAL STORIES FROM SPORTS, BUSINESS AND LIFE

Steve Rosenberg

Published by

GSD PRESS

www.makeboldthingshappen.com

For information about special discounts for bulk purchases or to contact the author, email sr@theteamgsd.com or visit www.makeboldthingshappen.com.

ISBN (paperback): 979-8-9873640-0-0
ISBN (ebook): 979-8-9873640-1-7

Editor: David Aretha
Book cover design: Joe Zeff, Joe Zeff Design, Inc.
Book interior design: Christy Day, Constellation Book Services
Publishing consultant: Martha Bullen, Bullen Publishing Services

Printed in the United States of America

This book is dedicated to my mother, Marcia. As you will read about inside, she died when I was seven years old. She was a dedicated schoolteacher who believed strongly in education. I often wonder what she would think of me, but one thing I'm certain is that she'd be incredibly proud that I wrote this book.

Contents

Introduction

I've been blessed to have had a wonderful career. From the time I was a young boy, I was determined to work in some capacity in the sports world. Of course as a younger version of myself, I'd imagined it would be on the field—like so many other young boys and girls. Oh, the dream of hitting the game-winning home run in the World Series would not come to be, but as I got older I realized there was indeed another path forward into the sports world and that was on the business side.

At that time the business part of sports was still relatively simple and not filled with complex television deals and licensing and merchandising rights fees, and certainly nobody could imagine what an NIL deal would look like. But as I committed to this career I realized that I was going to do everything it took to get myself into a position to work for a team and begin my ascension up the ladder and make my name in the sports world.

I was able to have a solid and fulfilling career that led me to many other unique projects in entertainment, hospitality, and nonprofit. Along my unplanned journey, I became the guy who was always able to make something happen—oftentimes when a door had already been closed. I had built a contact list of thousands and thousands and was always quickly able to connect people and to problem solve. In another life, I'd have been a great advisor to a United States senator. The people I met along the way taught me the journey is the most fun part. Winning awards, accomplishing goals, completing difficult tasks all have great rewards associated with them, but the journey is the key.

I am a serial networker. That is my true great quality in life. Follow-up is like a religion to me. I set a goal every week of whom

I'm going to connect with and in what form. My greatest pleasures have come from connecting two people who didn't know each other and watching a new great relationship build and seeing great things happen. That has been my gift to society so far.

In the next few hours of reading, I hope you find the stories you are going to read interesting, inspirational, and intriguing. There are many books out there offering words of encouragement and self-help. I don't see this book as a traditional title in that regard. What it is is a fun look at how to respond when you hear the word "no," now to deal with great adversity, and, most importantly, how to live your life meeting and working with a wide variety of people. The world is filled with so many interesting and terrific people. Consider it your job to go out and meet as many as possible – Make Bold Things Happen. You will be glad you did.

CHAPTER ONE

Act Like You've Been There Before

We are all faced with choices. Often these choices come quickly and we have to rely on our experience to determine how to act or respond. Hopefully we have been put in situations where we can quickly draw on what Malcolm Gladwell refers to as our 10,000 hours. He talks about the need to spend 10,000 hours doing anything for it to become habitual in nature. However, sometimes the situation is new to us and we have to quickly make a decision that could define us for a long period of time. This chapter will show you how I dealt with a situation in a humorous way.

On my first day of my very first job while I was still a full-time college student, I woke up that morning as excited as I could possibly be to attack the working world and explore the incredible opportunities that would be presented to me. As a naive and inexperienced 21-year-old, I knew I had a great deal to learn, but I was approaching this new era of my life with unbridled confidence, enthusiasm, and a zest to learn.

I also knew that there were several keys to success. Traits I'd observed from successful people growing up in Pittsburgh and as a student at the University of Maryland. While I never had a mentor growing up, there were clearly people I had admired and looked up to; people I wanted to emulate. These people all had various personalities and approaches toward others I had been observing.

Having begun work as a paperboy in the Squirrel Hill area of Pittsburgh at the age of 13, I learned about responsibility and dealing with people at an early age. Back in 1978, paper routes were handled on foot, carrying a shoulder bag, and walking from house to house to not only deliver the daily paper but to go to each home once a week to collect payment for that week's service. As a 13-year-old, going door to door to collect money from adults was not an easy task. However, I quickly figured out that good service and a smile would lead me to extra tips. I figured how hard is it to smile, show up on time, and use the magic words "please and thank you"?

So with all this incredible knowledge, wisdom, and know-how, I was certain that I would be a big success at my first "real" job. One that required a coat and tie, dress pants, and carrying a bag that included more than my lunch each day. However, I woke up that morning incredibly nervous because one thing was certain—I really didn't know what to expect or how to interact in a true office environment.

Fortunately for me, my first job was working for the professional basketball team in the Washington, DC metropolitan area—then called the Washington Bullets. The Bullets were just seven years removed from winning the NBA championship in 1978 and losing in the Finals a year later. This was a team that had a very good decade in the 1970s, but the 1980s would see them flail in mediocrity. Anyone who understands sports, especially team sports, knows that working for a team that doesn't make the playoffs, has a losing record, and plays in front of paltry home crowds is not a recipe for great success off the court either.

But the record didn't matter to me, nor did their history or the future. I had one goal in mind for my future and that was to become the commissioner of the NBA. (Spoiler alert, it hasn't happened yet!!) As a sports administration major, I was the happiest person in the world on this mid-September day as I was about to begin what was certain to be a long, successful, and, of course, storied career in sports.

Because I am perhaps the most on-time person I know, I arrived at the office at Capital Centre in Landover, Maryland, more than 25 minutes before I was due in. I am notorious for early arrivals as punctuality is one of the seven great attributes I will describe later in this book. I'm the guy who gets to the airport three hours in advance—so early, in fact, my family now refuses to arrive with me. We meet at the gate at this point.

So I showed up, parked in what seemed to be a perfectly acceptable but not obnoxious parking spot, and gathered my briefcase filled with three pens, a notebook, a sandwich, and my copy of *Street & Smith's NBA Guide* from the prior season. Back in the pre-internet days, these books were where you could find all the important and relevant information relating to players, teams, and the league.

I began my walk to the front door of the administrative offices, opened the door, and began walking toward the woman sitting at the reception desk. She had dark hair and was seated at a traditional reception style desk. She was older than I was, but at that point everyone was older than me. I guessed her to be about fifty years old and I still recall her wearing a headset on top of her well-styled hair. I introduced myself, told her who I was working for and what I was going to be doing. In my head this all sounded pretty good, but she sat there smiling at me as I must have sounded like a nervous new employee. However, we struck up a nice conversation and at that instance, I knew she was going to be an important person in my journey with the Bullets.

She told me she wasn't certain where my boss intended to have me seated, but she was expecting me and commented on my early arrival as she told me most of the staff didn't arrive until close to 9:30 a.m. I was there at 8:35 a.m. She directed me back to where my boss's office was and explained to me that this was a new space for him as his office changed just last night. As I entered his office to wait, it was clear that he had not worked in this space as most of his belongings were still not in place.

So I began walking and pacing and eventually noticed the morning's *Washington Post* sitting on his desk, crisply folded and waiting for him to page through. For some reason, I decided it would be a good idea for me to sit at his desk and await his arrival, and I then committed the sin of opening the paper and reading the sports page, thereby making this paper somewhat used. If you have ever enjoyed the pleasure of a great morning newspaper, the thrill of turning the pages for the first time is important. Reading a section that has already been opened, folded, and then re-closed just doesn't have the same appeal. And, as a former newspaper man myself—of course, on the delivery side of the process—I knew the importance of the morning paper.

Nevertheless, I opened the paper and read about the happenings from the day and night before. I got about a page or two in and out of the corner of my eye I saw someone who looked like they worked in operations walking toward the office. I began to panic because I was sitting at my boss's desk, reading his paper, and I had no idea who anyone was. So for some reason I decided to pick up the phone on his desk. Keep in mind, the phone hadn't been ringing and I had nobody to call, but I picked it up anyway. To make matters weirder, I began having a conversation with a pretend person on the other line!! So as I was having this conversation, the man appeared at the foot of the door, and I made eye contact with him. I put up my index finger signaling "Gimme one second." So I was on this fake call, probably taking credit for something that hadn't really happened, and I decided I better end it.

So I finally hung up and I looked at the man in the doorway and said, "Hi—can I help you?" He looked at me bewildered and amused and said, "Yeah, I'm here to hook up the phone." I was aghast and embarrassed and had only milliseconds to think of what to say, so for some reason I asked, "This phone?" He nodded affirmatively. I then said, "This phone works fine." He just looked at me, knowing I was completely full of crap, and turned and walked away.

Now here I was on my first day, arriving too early, sitting at the boss's desk, reading his paper, and I now turned away the engineer who was supposed to make sure his phone worked before my boss arrived!! So I got up, refolded the paper as best I could, and sat back on the visitors' side of the desk waiting for my boss to arrive.

About ten minutes later (the longest ten minutes of my life at this point), he walked in, grunted hello at me, mumbled something about traffic on the Beltway, and sat down at his desk. First, he glanced at his paper and realized it had been read, but he didn't say a word. Then he picked up his phone to make a call and it didn't work. He looked at me and asked, "Why the f**k isn't my phone hooked up?"

Eventually they all had quite a laugh on my account, and for the better part of the next year, I was called Bell (for Alexander Graham Bell). But I quickly turned this embarrassing moment into an opportunity both to relationship build and to network with people across the various departments. At that juncture, I had two ways to move forward:

I could wallow in self-pity and feel sorry for myself for acting like a dope and letting everyone tease me, or I could start laughing at myself along with them, get to know people's names and their job functions, and feel part of the team.

This gave me a quick way to get to know everyone. This is key in any environment in which you work, live, or play. Getting to know people, their stories, and most importantly their names is the number one rule of success.

Throughout this book, I'm going to give you tips I've learned along the way in amassing thousands and thousands of contacts from all walks of life and from many industries. The key to success in anything you do is knowing who to call, when to call, and what to say. Think about this: How many times have you been involved in a conversation that starts with one party asking, "Do you know anyone who...?"

You can fill in the blank for the industry, job function, or area. You've heard of the saying, (add a space here) "I got a guy for that" or "I know a guy who can...." Fortunately, in today's world, "guy" is often replaced with "woman" or "person." But the key here is being one degree away from knowing who can help you solve your issue(s) or help those you work with get answers to questions.

After all, getting shit done in an effective and timely manner is one of the great keys to success in life. Learning this early and developing good habits is critical.

CHAPTER TWO

Insights into In-Person Networking

This topic will either excite you or scare you. People are not always comfortable in large group settings where meeting new people is a primary objective. Here I try to show you examples of why networking is so critical as well as tips and tricks for how to "work a room."

The dictionary definition of NETWORKING is *the action or process of interacting with others to exchange information and develop professional or social contacts*. I believe this is a very accurate and functional definition and one that I would agree with. One would think this is simple, easy, and exciting. However, to an introvert the idea of interacting with others can be scary, uneasy, and anything but fun. Think about this scenario. You are asked to go to a big event to represent your organization and there is only one ticket available. You are not able to decline the invitation as your boss's boss will be there too.

Now in addition to wondering what you need to wear and who is going to be there, you have to figure out how to navigate a room full of mostly strangers and mingle your way through. You can't leave early because you need to report back to your boss and because your boss's boss will be there; it is crucial that you are soon networking and talking. Next to public speaking, this is one of the scarier things for people to do in life.

There are two types of people in this situation. The first group is those who are naturally gifted at navigating a room full of strangers. They are articulate, interesting, funny, and either authentic or give the appearance of being so. The second group is those who must work up the nerve to begin a conversation with a stranger. Often the first detour is to the bar while thinking this might take the edge off of conversing with this group of people you don't know and might not ever want to know. However, alcohol is not the answer to this question. In 2019, The first official random sample by The Myers-Briggs Company showed introverts made up 50.7 percent and extroverts 49.3 percent of the United States general population. I was surprised to see these percentages as I would have guessed introverts would have been a much higher percentage.

So how do you begin to navigate this situation and begin having conversations with people? I have a few tricks that I've used that work virtually every time I'm in a room of strangers. First you should know I am an introvert. I work hard to act as an extrovert, but I am not comfortable in these situations. My first stop is always the men's room. I need to make sure I am ready to go, and I have to look in the mirror to make sure I am presentable—whatever I'm wearing has to work.

The next step is to reach into the pocket for a mint. Not a piece of gum—nobody wants to talk to anyone chewing gum!! Grab a mint and make sure your breath is as fresh as can be. By the way, if you don't have any mints and are ever offered one from somebody, take it. They are offering because you need it!!

Then think of something that puts a smile on your face—your kids, siblings, significant other, favorite sports team, the money you just won on your last wager…whatever. Get your groove on and walk into the room like you are the person everyone is waiting for. Survey the room and focus on one or two people who seem to be in the same position as you. Whatever room you walk into, there are dozens of people at the same event, alone and looking to find someone they can begin to talk to and form their own small group around. These groups usually grow, and before you know it, you have met a bunch of people.

This is one way to prepare for these events. Now you've met a few people, and it becomes easier and easier to meet others. Oftentimes, the power is in the group dynamic. So take your newfound friends and go meet others. If some is good, more is better. Cast the widest net possible and do your best to conquer the majority of that room.

While you are there, take note of some of the other types of people in the room:

The Phantom Phone Call Person: Do you think I'm the only person to ever conduct a fake call? Clearly, I didn't invent this stall tactic, and now with the advent of cell phones it's even easier to take fake calls anywhere and everywhere. Plus add in earphones and you will absolutely see a few people in the corner or in the hallway on the phone pretending to take some very important call but really doing everything possible to avoid making eye contact with people in the room and developing new relationships.

The Waver: Watch this person who walks into the room and immediately begins waving at people to appear as if they know others. Typically this person will walk directly to the bar or in any other direction of their alleged friend, but they want you to know they know somebody.

The Phone Call Waver: This is an experienced and well-disciplined procrastinator. This person is combining the first two techniques into one. Take a fake call, but as you are on the phone wave every few minutes to someone in the back of the large room to give the appearance of multitasking. "Hey—be right there as soon I get off this super-important call."

There are so many anxious and nervous people. But why and for what reason? Is it that hard to walk up to another human being and say, "Hello, how are you? My name is Steve—what's yours and what's your connection to this group?" Bam—so simple and so easy. Perhaps if we were still kids on the playground, and we could organize a game of tag, it would be easier to get to know each other in the room. But alas, asking hundreds of dressed-up adults to join in the game of tag and then running around trying to determine who is "it" just won't work. Make yourself "it" and tag others with meaningful and interesting conversation. Be inquisitive and ask about the other person. You know why? People love to talk about themselves. But be an active listener and wait for tidbits of information that will let you know how long you want to invest in the conversation and in what direction you want to point things. A simple "Wow, that is really interesting. Tell me how you got into this role." Bingo—you're now free to eat your food, sip your drink, or if you are really good, pay attention and gaze over the room to see who else is there and where you want to head next.

The bottom line is that networking takes time and effort. But like anything in life that is worth pursuing, the easy way typically doesn't pay off. Think of these types of things as if you were a woodpecker who ended up in a petrified forest!! What are your choices—you must take your time and wait for opportunity. This is how life is. Then when you see an opening, you have to pounce—like a hobo on a ham sandwich. Jump on that thing and use your muscle, finesse, pizazz, and personality to get all that you can.

Eventually you are going to find yourself with a vast network of people you are able to call on. Your goal should always be to be able to make one phone call and find your answer. Whatever the question and whatever the issue in front of you is, think about who you know, where you met them, and how you can go about reaching out and connecting or re-connecting.

Fortunately in today's digitally dominated age, networking and keeping in touch has become so much easier than it ever has been.

From Facebook to LinkedIn, there are many great ways to connect and stay in contact. From a business perspective, LinkedIn has become a go-to business networking tool for so many. This platform allows you to grow your network by connecting with those folks who are connected to your network. You can see who your contacts know, what their business is, where they are located, and how you may be mutually beneficial to each other.

Later we will get into DOs and DON'Ts with LinkedIn, but just know that these tools help you in a plethora of ways and give you opportunities to grow professionally.

CHAPTER THREE

Those People You Meet Who Make an Impression

Everyone has a great story. The more time you take to meet new people, the more stories you will learn. It will also become easier to meet new people as you will want to hear their stories and their journeys of how you both ended up in the same room at the same time.

Throughout your early life, you will meet people who will undoubtedly make an impression on who you are, who you will become, and who you don't want to be like. Life is a continuous experimental and learning process of the greatest social exercise possible. I remember as a young boy watching the television show *Taxi*. In one episode, one of the characters is asked to babysit another character's children. The first character has no children, knows nothing about children, and is trying to just get by. When asked by the young people he's asked to babysit to read a story to them, he simply says, "A prince was born, he lived, he died." To this day, I repeat that line with friends or in settings where I know it will get a laugh.

I bring this up for two important reasons. The first is, lives aren't that simple. Yes, we are born, we live, and then we die, but between being born and dying there are so many roads taken, roads passed by, and roads we wished we could have endeavored upon. We can wonder all day what would have happened if we did this or hadn't done that. But we are who we are for a reason, and the stories we can tell, the people we have met, and the things we've seen and done are what make us who we are.

In this book, I'm going to introduce you to several people whom I admire and who have made an impression on me for a variety of reasons. Their personality, their ability to get shit done, the way they network and/or follow up, or just because they are really interesting. Isn't life so much more fun when we meet people who are indeed interesting and fun?

Some of the people I will introduce you to will have entire chapters devoted to them while others may get quick mentions in stories with notes on what impact they had on me and how they affected the way I go about the hard work I'm trying to let you in on.

But no matter what, pay attention. Life is an amusement park. Some rides require you to be a certain height to board and others are open for anyone. Pick and choose carefully who you see, when you see them, and why you agree to see them. Think of your network like a target. You have a series of rings. The closest to the bullseye are your best friends and closest allies. From there, everyone in each ring is another degree separated from you.

I can think of so many great characters and people I've met throughout my life. Generally speaking, I know where I first encountered them and what, over time, I learned from them—good or bad. You see, that is what the key is. Everyone teaches you something; it's up to you to learn what it is.

My mother passed away when I was seven years old. She died from hepatitis due to a lanced boil from a scalpel not properly sterilized. In today's world, that would be worth millions. I didn't find this out until later in life, but back in 1972, people didn't sue doctors. In fact, people didn't sue many people. The world was far less litigious than it is today. The world was a lot of things less back then. Less contentious, less dangerous, less hectic, less crowded, and less complicated. No need to get into how the world worked back then as you all know about it.

But when a young child loses a parent, especially a mother, everything changes. If you haven't gone through this, it's incredibly difficult to put into words. However, your entire perspective on the world changes. How you view things, how people view you, and how you think people view you. I spent decades not talking about her death, discussing it with nobody, and this impacted me greatly. I don't know, nor do I truly understand psychology or sociological impact, but I believe I was an extrovert as a young child. The stories I've seen, home movies I've watched, and pictures I have looked through all suggest I was quite outgoing and not afraid to put myself out there.

I am certain that after May 24, 1972, all of that changed. The world took the most important thing I had away from me and my young brother, who was only two years old. How would I cope, move forward, and deal with the world? How would I see things now? Time would tell, but there was a series of events that totally altered the course of my life, and this is one of those major "What would have happened if this didn't happen?" moments.

After she passed away, we moved in with my father's parents, my grandparents. Two wonderful people who were just slightly younger than I am now, which is really hard for me to believe. Later that summer my father moved to Columbus, Ohio, to take a new job. I was too young to understand any of it, but there I was, living with my grandparents in a new neighborhood, going to a new school, needing to make all new friends, and trying to comprehend it all. I was beginning my networking at that moment. That first day of school at Colfax Elementary in Squirrel Hill was my true test. Problem was, there was no bar, no drinks to be had, and no practice rounds. This was it…. It was on.

Within weeks I met who would become most of my best friends in life. Friends I still have to this day and whom I talk to by phone or text each day of my life. I still remember that first day of school and my grandmother walking me in—fortunately, I was a giant seven-year-old, and I towered over most of the kids, so I had that going for me. But any question about my mom or my parents would just go ignored. I don't think I really discussed my mother's passing, and if asked about my father, I am pretty sure I just said he traveled a lot. I don't know why I didn't discuss it, but I didn't. I really think I didn't want to make other people feel bad or sorry for me, so I just let it go. Clearly not the right thing to do, but it's what I did.

I became very quiet at home, usually making as much time as I could for my baby brother, who was too young to go to school and really had no friends. In my mind, he was my responsibility, and I was going to do everything I could to protect him from any more evil. I didn't know how I was going to do that, but I was. I had two grandfathers—the one I lived with and my mother's father (the one who raised her; her natural father had died when she was just a baby). I loved them both, but they were from a different era. My uncle, my father's brother, was my defacto mentor, but he lived in New York City, and I didn't see him enough.

You want to talk about times gone by? With my father living in Columbus, my brother and I would take the Greyhound bus from Pittsburgh *alone* to Columbus. My grandmother, who never drove a car, took us on the bus to the Greyhound station, where she purchased tickets for us. We'd be the first two in line so we could always get the seats behind the driver. She'd walk us onto the bus and say something to the driver that we couldn't hear but probably went something like, "Please take good care of them." Keep in mind, this bus was not direct to Columbus. We stopped in really great places like Wheeling, West Virginia, and Zanesville, Ohio. These are the cities where Freddy Krueger and Jason Voorhees lived. But we'd get off the bus, go buy a snack or two, and walk back on. A seven-year-old and a two-year-old, then an eight-year-old and a three-year-old, and so on. Our dad met us in Columbus and then we'd do the same thing on the way back. Can you imagine putting your kids on the Greyhound bus to go anywhere right now? Kids today aren't allowed to walk to school!!

All of this helped shape who I was and who I became. I learned how to talk to strangers and who not to talk to, and fear became something we didn't think about. You also saw good in many people. There was always a helpful adult willing to make sure we had what we needed or to remind us to get back to the bus as the rest stop was coming to an end. I can't imagine what it would be like to see two young boys seven and under on a bus alone and what I would want to do to help.

Back in those days, we called (and we still do) everyone by a nickname or by what they did. Everyone had a name. If we couldn't come up with a name that described you, we would just shorten (or lengthen) your last name. But it all made sense and it was all with purpose.

Everything we did, every activity we participated in, every game we played made us who we were and what we became. If we played a game, we kept score, and someone won and someone lost. You learned how to lose without crying and how to win without being a dick. If you lost every game, there were no rewards for you—you didn't get an eight-inch bronze statue that said you were here. You made friends, created memories, and ended up with a shirt of some kind that you still wish you had.

This is what we knew and what we did. It's how we learned to interact and deal with other human beings. Technology has taken so much of that away, and we must be diligent in our communication efforts. When I meet a person in their twenties or thirties who has outstanding verbal and written communication skills, I am so impressed. I fear this will soon become a lost art, and to me, it is one of the great skills that life teaches you.

As you think about communicating and interacting with other people, consider this for today's younger generations. In prior decades and mostly before mobile phones, you called people in their homes. Typically a parent or guardian would answer, and you would be forced to make conversation—polite conversation. "Hello, Mrs. Smith. Is Johnny home?" Then Mrs. Smith might confirm his affirmative or negative presence, but first she might inquire as to how you are, how school is, and how your family is. These small but simple interactions piled on top of each other became the foundation of how we became adults. How we learned to deal with those older than us. How we learned to respect our elders and have meaningful conversations. For today's young people, this is difficult—why pick up the phone and talk to someone when a text or DM might suffice? Why spell a word in its entirety when LOL works quite well?

The bottom line here is, take your time, spend some time, and learn how to communicate effectively. There is nothing more important or more valuable than the written and spoken word—especially when it is authentic and comes from the heart.

Back Home to Jerusalem

The road isn't easy for most people. What we see on television or read about in books is usually based on fiction and not reality. Dreams are not always achieved, but when they do become reality, the stories are sometimes amazing. People who overcome incredible odds often become leaders and inspirations for many.

For the majority of my life, international travel seemed as likely as going to the moon. I didn't even travel to Florida until I was in my twenties. The thought of going to Europe, Asia, or the Middle East was not even possible as a child. At some point, you just write off certain things as a wish, a hope, or a dream. Well, eventually, my ticket was cashed and I was able to travel abroad with a trip to Europe. It was an amazing experience and beyond anything I could have ever imagined.

Growing up in the United States, we are blessed to have so many assets and opportunities that it isn't necessary to dream of life in any other place. In fact, people from all over the world have been immigrating to the United States to seek those same freedoms and liberties we have been enjoying since the signing of the Constitution in 1787. Even today, talk of immigration overtakes the news on many days. This isn't a political book, so I will spare you any discussion regarding legal vs. illegal immigration and the merits of coming to this country. However, so many people across the globe wake up every morning in peril and poverty. There are nations on this planet so poor that people dream every day of escaping to a better life. Most never get that chance, and that is why so many are willing to risk their lives, leaving everything behind, to find whatever there is at the end of the rainbow.

When I first met Sigal Kanotopsky, she had just moved to the United States from Israel. She had lived in Israel since 1983, when she emigrated from Gondar, Ethiopia. Sigal's story is the ultimate one of perseverance, determination, hard work, faith, and inspiration. Sigal is regional director of the Northeast for the Jewish Agency for Israel, also known as JAFI. The Jewish Agency is the largest nonprofit in the Jewish community and one of the largest in the world. Most people know JAFI as the organization responsible for helping Jews across the globe make "Aliyah" (become citizens of Israel). The organization does many other good and important pieces of work, but this is what they have become known for around the globe. Recently, JAFI has been instrumental in helping displaced Jewish citizens of Ukraine become citizens of Israel via the Aliyah program.

Forty years ago, as Ethiopia was deteriorating and it was becoming impossible for Jews to live there, concerted and oftentimes covert operations were put into place to take Ethiopian Jews out of their native land and to Israel to make Aliyah and begin a new life filled with education, employment, and opportunity. The original mission was called "Operation Moses" and it saw over 8,000 Ethiopian Jews land in Israel in secrecy—the kind of story you see in movies and read about in books.

Sigal, who was just a young child in the early 1980s, was told by her family one day they were leaving Gondar and would make a long and laborious trek to Sudan. In Ethiopia, Jews talked incessantly about "going home" to Jerusalem. This was what so many dreamed about and hoped for. Shabbat (Friday sundown to Saturday sundown) is the most important time in Gondar for the Jewish community, and the families would sit together and talk about the rivers that overflowed with milk and honey as legend had it. What other great opportunities awaited them in Jerusalem? They probably never would find out. They didn't even realize there were other cities in Israel like Tel Aviv, Haifa, or even Nazareth. They knew Jerusalem and that was where they wanted to be.

One day, Sigal and her six siblings were told they were leaving and to take whatever they could carry and leave the rest. All they knew was, they were going to Sudan. There were rumors about Jerusalem, but as to how and when… Could it really be possible? Even as a young child, Sigal had to have faith and hope that this could ultimately occur.

For close to four weeks they marched—moving only at night when they could not be seen, and they rested during the days. This was not an easy trek, and they had to be careful. This was the ultimate "get shit done" experience, and their grit and determination were going to win out. Eventually they found their way to Sudan. However, that did not ensure safe passage out and to Israel. All this left them with more questions, but now, instead of living in their home in Gondar, they sat together in a refugee camp in Sudan with more disease than there was food. Elder adults and young babies died among them from starvation or an inability to remain healthy in the refugee camp environment. How long would they be there, and what would happen next? Information was scarce. What they didn't know at the time was that both the Israeli and American governments, along with key NGOs, were working behind the scenes to help get the Ethiopians out of Sudan and on a plane to safe harbor in Israel.

So they were afforded basic food and very necessary medicine. In addition to everything else, they were never allowed to mention anything about being Jewish. They were simply refugees from Ethiopia seeking a better life.

As they observed the Jewish festival of Passover while in the camp, they realized they were living out a real and modern-day exodus and a literal passing over of all the Jewish Ethiopians. If only they could survive, the thanks they would give and the new meaning their lives would take... And Passover would become a true inspiration and a real story to be told.

Eventually their names were called, and there was a plane waiting for them. They did not know what this meant or where the plane would take them. Information was sparse and communication very infrequent. But they had no choice—they had come this far, and it was time to take the next step. Was it possible this plane would take them back to Ethiopia? Absolutely—at that point, anything was possible. But they kept their spirits high, boarded the plane, and hoped for the best.

As they sat on the plane, one thing was very noticeable—even for a young child like Sigal. It was perfectly quiet. Even the babies weren't making any noise. Everyone was frozen in fear as to what was going to happen next. Most closed their eyes and prayed. They held hands and held each other. There was no meal service and certainly no entertainment—not on this flight. This was a "close your eyes and pray" type of mission.

Eventually the silence was broken by the captain, who said, "Welcome to Ben Gurion Airport." You would think this would have been met with an eruption of cheers and cries of joy. However, most if not all of the passengers didn't know what Ben Gurion Airport was or even where it was. Finally someone told them, "It's Jerusalem." Now the truth is that Ben Gurion is in Tel Aviv and about an hour's drive to Jerusalem. But they got the picture and learned quickly they were finally home. They did it—the teamwork made the dream work. Of course, this new home would not be easy and was filled with new types of bumps, potholes, and forks in the road.

For example, nobody in Sigal's family spoke Hebrew—the main language of the State of Israel. Her father didn't have a job, and they didn't have a home—important details to give yourself a good and happy life. But the most important thing to everyone in that place was that they were no longer in Ethiopia or Sudan—they were home in Israel. Whatever their new beginnings were and whatever obstacles lay in front of them would pale in comparison to the journey of the past six-plus months when everything had been in doubt—including their survival.

They left the plane, and every single one of the passengers fell to their knees and kissed the ground. I've never experienced that feeling before, and I think it is probably safe to assume that most of you haven't either. Think of the joy and elation that would cause you to do something like that. The peril you must have overcome and gratitude you must have felt for being wherever you were at that time.

But it was time for their next journey. Fortunately they were together, safe, and reasonably healthy. The State of Israel was ready for them and had absorption centers operating where these new immigrants would learn the language and become part of the Israeli culture as soon as possible. They found themselves in the town of Ashkelon. There they would spend the necessary time learning to become Israeli. No longer were they Ethiopians—they were Israelis.

Eventually they were moved up to a town near Nazareth, and Sigal remembers their first Shabbat. She presumed everything in Israel would be shut down and quiet as it was back in Gondar on Friday nights. However, she learned that not all Jews are observant, and Israel is filled with many other types of people who don't observe Shabbat each week. However, that first Shabbat in Israel was incredibly inspiring and moving and something she still holds near and dear.

Eventually her older siblings were separated from the younger ones and sent off to boarding school, where they would become more indoctrinated into Israeli education and culture. This was confusing and not easy for Sigal and her other young siblings, but they learned to accept that this was the way it was going to be. However, life became even more challenging when her father passed away just a year and a half into their new life in Israel. Was it the journey? Would he have lived longer in Gondar? Nobody knows. But he was able to fulfill an incredible dream that became a new reality for his family. He gave them a wonderful new life with infinite possibilities to succeed and to live. This gift he left is something that Sigal understands and carries with her.

Eventually Sigal began to attend a very observant and religious school. The kind of school where going into the army was not generally looked upon favorably. For every 100 graduates, maybe four go into the army to serve their country. This, however, was not an option for Sigal. She was determined to serve and do it proudly. She graduated and joined the army and attended officer training, rising to the rank of lieutenant.

She then went on to get both her undergraduate and graduate degrees in Israel and ultimately became the chief executive officer of Olim Be'yachad, an NGO acting to change perceptions and eliminate racism within Israeli society through employment and the media. Under Sigal's direction, the organization grew and received many honors and awards. Sigal was recognized with the Rappaport Prize for women leading breakthroughs, and she was selected as one of the 50 most influential leaders.

She then became vice president of development for MAOZ—a leadership organization in Israel where Sigal is an alumnus.

Eventually she knew she needed to work for the Jewish Agency and serve the diaspora in North America. Since the Jewish Agency was there for her and her family, it was crucial for her to carry on this important work. At this point, Sigal was married with four children of her own, and she knew the possibility existed that she might have to move to the United States for a period of time, but she hoped this would come to be. Someone she knew and admired in a position of great importance at the Jewish Agency reached out to her and told her about a great opportunity for her within the organization. Now was her time. She told her family it was incumbent upon them to serve as emissaries for Israel and go to the United States to help people understand that Israelis come in different shapes, sizes, colors, and even religions. While her time in the United States is defined for a short period of only a few years, she's already made a remarkable impact.

Sigal has built a network of allies helping her do the work she cares most about—in Hebrew, it is called Tikkun Olam (repair the world). This can take on many forms and meanings, but to Sigal, it is simple: show the big picture of Israel and all of the advances the country has made and contributed to the rest of the world. Lead by example and help people understand the complicated situation taking place daily in the Middle East. But she brings incredible perspective and knowledge mixed with passion and intelligence and kindness.

She may be in the United States, but she truly is back home in Jerusalem every day of her life.

Sigal did everything in her power to Make Bold Things Happen. She has become an insatiable networker with incredible follow-up. Her dogged determination and desire to succeed has allowed her to not only follow her dreams, but to exceed anything she ever could have imagined.

CHAPTER FIVE

Life Is a Participatory Activity

I have a very dear friend who always says, "Get Yours," whenever he leaves a conversation. He is an acclaimed author himself and writes about confidence. He is right when he talks about getting yours. If you don't go get yours, someone else will. Wake up and carpe diem—seize the day. The day will not seize you. Read through these pages to see how and why waking up, answering the bell, and fighting hard each day is so important.

You will meet many people in this life, most of whom are working hard to get to the point of retirement. That comes in different forms and at different times for different people. Most people seek retirement as the comfortable part of life—when life gets fat and it's time to relax and chill and reap the comforts of your hard work.

But is there such a thing as actual comfort? And if there is, what does it look like? What is your purpose for being here? What intentions do you have regarding leaving your mark? Do you want to be remembered or be just one of those people who did what they could, worked hard, retired, and then died? Remember, "A prince was born, he lived, he died." Seems like a simple enough life, but what fun did the prince have? What was the prince's name, and what was his legacy? Sure, we are talking about a prince, but what prince? The singer formerly known as? The prince of some foreign land? Nobody knows and worse, nobody cares.

Back in March 2005, *The Wall Street Journal* published a front-page story titled, "Trophy Overload." I was the featured person in the story because I had finally tried to put an end to participation trophies in our very large youth baseball organization. Participation trophies were beginning to cause unnecessary wussification among our youth. Here, Little Johnny, you showed up, so you get a trophy. By the way, you may not have even shown up all year, but you showed up on the day we are handing out these six-inch bronze statues so you can have one to show everyone you've gotten an award for nothing.

There is no question in my mind that these trophies began a negative trend that we are paying for today. Entitled kids have grown up to be entitled adults. The participation trophy generation, with their snack schedules, equal play rule, and everybody-wins mentality, has learned nothing about winning with dignity and losing with grace. The only possible way to understand how good victory or success tastes and feels is to have experienced losing or failure. While too much failure is terrible, a little bit goes a long way in creating backbone, resilience, and fortitude. We all have heard the saying "What doesn't kill you makes you stronger." Unfortunately, something happened along the way. The helicopter parent generation began guarding you and forbidding you from being a kid. You weren't allowed to fail. You weren't allowed to fall from your bikes or scooters, and you certainly weren't allowed to climb a tree.

Moving forward, you have to understand that failure is not the opposite of success—it must be part of success. You must know how to fail. When you fall, you don't just lie there. You do as the song suggests—you pick yourself up, take a deep breath, dust yourself off, and start all over again.

This is so critically important. You cannot be afraid to fail, and you must not be embarrassed to lose. The Buffalo Bills lost not one, not two, not three, but *four* consecutive Super Bowls. What nobody talks about is, to lose four straight Super Bowls, you actually have to be successful enough to make it to four straight. Ask a Detroit Lions fan if they would like one chance to play on the NFL's biggest stage. Celebrate the success—you work hard and spend hours looking to figure out where the road to success begins.

However, comfort is not the end goal. You should strive for a fulfilling life of purpose and then attack that purpose with all the vigor you can muster. Be like a hobo on a ham sandwich and attack like you haven't eaten in days. Most people get involved in things for one of three reasons:

- Meaning
- Significance
- Lifestyle

To be clear, significance is the extent that something matters while meaning is the symbolic value. Lifestyle speaks to how anything impacts you. As an example, say you buy a Mercedes S Class. Why did you make this purchase? First, because you always wanted a prime luxury automobile, and second, the S Class tells everyone you have arrived. Driving an S Class may also (third) impress your friends or significant other. The S Class has checked not one of the three boxes but actually all three. There are many other examples, and you should think about how meaning, significance, and lifestyle fit into your own personal journey. But they matter, and it's up to you to figure out how and why.

One of the main reasons people choose to be comfortable is because it is much easier to just fit in. Rinse, wash, repeat.... Be part of life's assembly line, and don't make waves. History seldom remembers or recognizes the line workers, but it does recognize the leaders, the outliers, and those who weren't afraid to step outside and take chances.

Think about some of the world's great leaders and about some of the chances they took. In the chapters in this book, you will meet some people whom I admire who did just this. They aren't particularly famous. They haven't cured cancer, split the atom, or come up with a peace plan for the Middle East. But they are unapologetic, authentic risk-takers who are unabashedly outspoken on topics important to them.

They get networking and follow-up and are diligent in their efforts. They see the finish line and don't cruise to the end; they go full speed ahead until they've blown past the checkered flag. No is not a final answer, and they don't even understand "I don't know" or "maybe." They are grinders and hustlers who are determined to make some sort of difference in the world. I'm excited to introduce them to you.

I eventually won the argument about participation trophies. But had you been in the room during the discussions, you would have thought I suggested we take the kids out to an alley and drop them into dumpsters like it was trash day. My point was and remains: Do an outstanding job, get a reward. Pavlov taught his dog to salivate at the sound of a bell. I'm reasonably certain we could teach our human children to work hard to earn rewards.

I've always wondered what would happen if certain sports were played where the winner was the only one to receive any money. Winner takes all. Boxing, tennis, golf—in most individual sports, this could be fantastic. Imagine a boxing match where neither participant was guaranteed any money. The two pugilists fought each other until one was left standing, and that person took the purse. I'm not Pavlov and I don't play him on television, but I suspect the two combatants would go as hard as possible to win the fight.

Remember: Winning isn't everything but losing sucks. The great Vince Lombardi, one of the greatest football coaches of all time, said, "Winning isn't everything; it's the only thing." And of course, the legendary fictional character Ricky Bobby from *Talladega Nights* said, "If you're not first, you're last." There are so many quotes about winning, but they all say the same thing. If you are going to participate in an activity—go all out. Play to win. If you don't win, look your opponent in the eye, congratulate them, and move on and attempt to figure out what you must do to get better. Is it 10,000 more hours of practice? Is it more training, more learning—what is it? Nobody has ever won everything they've ever done, but many have won with practice and experience. At the end of the day, nobody should get a trophy for just showing up.

CHAPTER SIX

Hail to the Chief

You are going to find yourself in situations where you are punching above your weight. This could involve dating someone you never thought would say yes, buying a house you didn't think you could afford, or attending a party with people you deem fancier than you. Here I talk about confidence and how to approach any situation where success is the only option even when the players seem bigger than you.

The president of the United States has been referred to as the "leader of the free world" and the most important person on earth. Basically a very high value has been placed on someone who, when you think about it, really came out on top in a popularity contest. The presidents of today trade on the value of those who came before them. Great Americans like George Washington, Abraham Lincoln, Harry Truman, John Kennedy, and Ronald Reagan.

When you look back at some of the accomplishments that have been attributed to the Oval Office, this brand equity is easily transferred from president to president. When the presidential motorcade pulls up, people get excited. The president owns sports star or rock star status. They get cheered, jeered, praised, and ridiculed. Their every move is watched, rewatched, reviewed, and analyzed. Why anyone would want this job is a question for another time—but truly, the answer is ego. What else can you do that gives you this much power? Nothing else even compares. Members of Congress are pretty important as are Supreme Court justices—but nothing compares (one would imagine) to being the president of the United States of America.

The job today has become slightly less impressive to some, but if you look at attendance numbers and influence ratings, the president is very significant. If the president had a Q score rating, I'd imagine it would be higher than any other person. A Q score is a measurement of familiarity for a person or brand in the United States. The higher the Q score, the more highly rated the person or brand is. This rating is heavily used by the advertising industry. I am guessing the president would be the ultimate pitch person if allowed by law!!

How many people get to be up close to either a sitting president or past president? There are only a couple of living humans who have occupied the Oval Office, so meeting with or talking to any of these people is almost as rare as meeting the current president. What do you say, what do you wear, and what is it like to be in the same room?

I have had the great pleasure of meeting or being in an intimate setting with four of the forty-six men who have held the title of president of the United States. That is a pretty high percentage, and the stories are actually interesting and fall into the category of making things happen.

In 2003, I was doing work with the National Constitution Center in Philadelphia in the Independence Mall near the Liberty Bell and Independence Hall. We were supposed to have our grand opening on July 4th of that year, with a series of extraordinary events including hosting both President William Jefferson Clinton and President George H. W. Bush. There was going to be a special VIP cocktail party for high-level donors and dignitaries to meet both presidents, including a receiving line and photograph opportunity with both of these distinguished gentlemen.

As one of the people in charge of the entire evening, including overseeing all security for the event, I knew I had my opportunity to get into the reception area and talk to these two before the festivities began. As I walked around the room, there stood both President Bush and President Clinton, standing and talking to each other. It's amazing the things you notice when you make your first observation of people, but both of these men were really big. The room was far from empty, and I wasn't sure what my move was going to be. So I walked up to the security guards and began a conversation. I also saw the lead agent from the Secret Service, whom I'd been dealing with, and gave him a nod and asked if all was good and if he needed anything. He told me all was okay, but I walked up to him anyway and just decided to go for it since I saw the photographer was already in the room.

I told him I never ask for photographs with celebrities, but I'd appreciate the opportunity to jump in with both of these distinguished gentlemen and get a picture that could be a storyteller for years to come. No problem, I was told, and I walked in between them. I called over to the photographer and told him to get his ass in gear as I couldn't keep the presidents waiting, which actually drew a laugh from President Clinton.

We lined up with me in the middle. This was a black-tie event, so I was in a tuxedo, but I opted for a gold tie and gold vest. Neither of these two men was wearing a tuxedo, so I really stood out. As I stood in the middle, I was shocked at how tiny I felt. I'm not a giant, but I never considered myself short. By far, I'm the shortest male in my family and always felt cheated by several inches. Combine that with my incredibly poor posture, and there I stood between President Clinton and President Bush who both stood well over six feet.

I was ready for the picture, and right before George the photographer got ready to snap the picture, President Clinton turned to me and said, "Man, that is a really nice tie—I really, really like that tie." I literally looked up at him and said, "Thank you, Mr. President, I like your tie." That made George Bush giggle, and then we took the picture. This was 2003, so I wasn't able to see the picture immediately. I had to wait several days to see if it even turned out. Can you imagine a twenty-something having to wait today for a picture of that magnitude? I was hopeful my eyes were open, and more importantly, that theirs were. I knew I generally took pretty solid photographs, but I couldn't speak for Bill and George. One would suspect they might have some experience.

I turned to both of them and shook their hands, thanked them for their service, and wished them a great evening. They asked what it was that I did and how I had such early access. I explained my role as overseer of logistics and security for the evening, and then they thanked me. I'm certain we could have had a lengthier conversation, but they were looking for some quiet time and only had about ten minutes before the other guests were going to arrive, and I wanted to make sure they had time to get something to eat and drink.

I made sure to walk over to my new friend from the Secret Service, whom I'd been working with for the previous couple of days, thanked him, and asked him if I could get him anything. Remember, you always thank the person at the door. It's one thing to thank the talent, but it's much more important to thank the person at the loading dock who opens the door for you. He told me he was fine, and I assured him I'd check in on him later and bring him and his crew dinner—which I did at the conclusion of the event. I had a great dinner packaged for them and told him where I'd put it so they could eat it later or take it with them. I have no idea if they ever ate it, but I know he appreciated the effort. Those are the efforts you put forth to take care of those who take care of you.

To this day, that photograph has a special place in my scrapbook of memories. I bring it out occasionally, and it does sit on a mantel in my office. With everything I have and all of the mementos, this is by far the piece that receives the most comments and questions. It doesn't matter whether I liked their politics; they held the highest office in the land, and I was able to talk to them briefly and sit in between them for a memorable photograph. These are the moments you work hard for. You put yourself in a position to be successful so that when opportunity appears, you are able to seize it and maximize any good fortune that comes your way. Not all good fortune comes as a financial reward—some are great memories, experiences, and stories.

In February 2022, a friend of mine living in Highland Beach, Florida, called to see if my wife and I wanted to have dinner at Mar-A-Lago. Donald Trump owned this estate in Palm Beach, Florida. Mar-A-Lago became a household name later in 2022 as it became the first presidential residence to be raided by the FBI, but that isn't relevant to this story.

The answer was an immediate yes, even though a 7 p.m. dinner in Palm Beach would mean leaving Miami Beach no later than four-thirty that afternoon in the hopes of being on time. And if you know me, tardiness is not only unacceptable but also a horrible trait. My friend called to give me the lowdown on where to pull in, what to wear, and what the basic rules of Mar-A-Lago are. It is a private club, and rules prevail in all circumstances. Additionally, former President Trump resides there, and it has massive security measures in place for arrival and while on property.

I was told to tell my wife that she was able to show either cleavage or knees, but not both. It was prime rib night and those were the rules. It seemed like an odd rule, but I relayed the message exactly as I'd heard it—cleavage or knees. My wife found this incredibly difficult to digest—not because she needed to show both but because she had never heard of such a dress code. So for the entire two-hour ride to Palm Beach, we were dissecting whether she was dressed appropriately. I was wearing a sports coat, an open-collar shirt, and pants (no jeans!!).

The ride to Palm Beach from Miami Beach during rush hour on a weekday can be quite tortuous, and my tolerance for traffic and bad drivers is very short. But we made it up in one piece and we pulled into this posh estate. As we pulled up to the security gate, I offered my name, and our vehicle began to get inspected, including underneath to determine the presence of any type of explosive device. We passed easily and were offered directions to the valet and were waved through. Our car was no slouch, but as we pulled up to the valet, I realized we may have been better off parking in the employee lot as every single car I saw was a Bentley, Rolls-Royce, or some other high-end luxury model.

After being escorted out of the car, we walked in and were greeted and directed to the restaurant, where we were told to wait for our hosts. Prior to heading out to that area, we stopped in the restroom since we'd been in the car for a couple of hours. I can't speak to the ladies' room, but the men's room was filled with pictures of President Trump in many different settings; most involved him playing golf. No matter where you looked, there he was.

There was a no-camera rule at Mar-A-Lago, but I did my best to sneak a few shots of the men's room before anyone else sauntered in. After washing up, I met my wife outside, and we walked to the bar. We each ordered a drink as we waited for our hosts. While talking and looking around at the women dressed in gowns and the men in coats and ties (highly unusual for South Florida), we began to hear the faint sound of clapping and cheering. For some reason, I said something stupid like "I guess it's someone's birthday" as I forget for a moment where we were. My wife turned to me and said, "We aren't at Olive Garden. Trump must be walking in." It never occurred to me that President Trump would be there or that he would be this close. Sure enough, there he was, walking in with Secret Service in front of and behind him. The crowd began to rise as he walked by, cheering and offering thumbs-up gestures. He was the king of the literal castle and he enjoyed every second. He walked directly past us and we made eye contact. I offered him my own thumbs-up. After all, this was his house, and that is the greeting he likes.

He sat down at the prime table in the center of the room, where he could be seen by every table. To be seated, you had to walk by his table. This seemed odd to me as it was not only a security issue but also a nuisance and bothersome detail. But it wasn't my decision and he was not a typical person. We were so dialed into his entrance, we didn't realize our hosts had arrived and were standing next to us with big smiles, asking us if we enjoyed the little show.

We were then asked if we were ready to go to our table. All I cared about at this juncture was how close we were going to get to the president. While I was anxious to catch up with my friends, I know that the show that is President Trump is not one that most get to enjoy. At this point, the president was joined by his son and his son's famous girlfriend. It was a real power table…and if one could just be a fly on the tablecloth!!

BAM!! We got the best seat in the house, one table away right in the center, and President Trump was just over my left shoulder. My only concern at this point was with the no-camera rule; how was I going to get this picture I needed? *Do I pretend to look at my email and take a selfie? Do I ask my wife to do so?* Everyone was looking right at the president, which means they were looking through me. Should I care? I might never be back again, and I was trying to seize the moment. I deliberated with myself for a few minutes while trying to engage in small talk with our hosts. Finally I decided to try the selfie route. It did not go very well—the pictures were blurry and I looked like Eddie Munster. I had to try again—another bad result. I put the phone away and tried to enjoy dinner and the incredible atmosphere, but you really just can't take your eyes off of this table with President Trump.

Finally, I got my wife to do her best, and we got a decent shot, which turned out to be pretty funny. It's a picture of me with President Trump right behind me. After I was successful with a decent picture, my friend pointed out the iPad on the table in front of the president. I glanced and saw it, and he explained to me that Trump was controlling the music. The president was the DJ that night. I found this odd because while I'm not a big music guy, I did notice there was no real flow to the music, and some songs were being played at a higher volume than others.

My buddy then said to me, "Here is what is going to happen soon.… He's going to play a Bocelli song and then out of that, he will go right into 'YMCA.'" I looked at him like, *C'mon, man*. Sure enough about eight minutes later, I heard some song by Andrea Bocelli and then right after that, the volume went up, and here came the Village People singing "YMCA." As soon as "YMCA" started, the entire restaurant went crazy—like a college bar crowd hearing their favorite song. People got up and started doing the YMCA dance.

President Trump was sitting at the table with two thumbs-up, swinging his arms in a dance-like manner, and everyone was giving him the thumbs-up back. Even one of the guests at the president's table (including the famous girlfriend) was up doing the YMCA dance. I looked at my wife, who was laughing as she couldn't believe what was happening. Finally, the song ended, the volume came down, and I don't recall what song came on next because I couldn't believe what I had just seen. The night was now complete. Former president and current DJ Donald Trump just had the entire Mar-A-Lago crowd dancing to the song "YMCA."

Over the course of the evening, the president was joined by a couple of other unidentified guests. Eventually his meal concluded, and he stood up to thunderous applause. He began his short walk back to his residence to another standing ovation. We had not yet had dessert, so I missed my opportunity to try to approach the table and say hello, but this was a most interesting evening dining close with the forty-fifth president of the United States.

After dinner, we toured the rest of the property, which was

absolutely incredible. Of all the investments Trump has made, this has to be at or near the top. He bought it for such a reasonable sum, and it is now worth hundreds and hundreds of millions of dollars if not more. While I didn't have the same personal interaction I had with Bush and Clinton, this was more fun and more memorable for a variety of reasons. While part of it was luck, I made my own luck by being able to be in the right spot at the right time.

As irony would have it, the following week we were at dinner at another restaurant in Miami and the first lady at the time, Jill Biden, was there having dinner with friends. It's really incredible to see leaders of our nation firsthand and in casual and natural settings. I did meet Joe Biden years earlier, but it was only for a short time and far less memorable.

No matter what happens, these memories will last forever. Make sure you make memories and have great stories to tell. Good, smart, funny, and authentic stories. If nothing else, your grandkids will think you are hilarious.

CHAPTER SEVEN

A Grandmother's Love

When NO isn't the answer you want or need, what do you do? This chapter will introduce you to a man who doesn't understand the definition of the words NO, CAN'T, or WON'T. How does he push through closed doors? Let's take a closer look.

Imagine showing up to high school as a freshman. It is a small high school with about 100 total people. You have been a baseball player your entire life up until this point and you want to try to play for the next four years. The problem is there is no baseball team. The school has football, boys' basketball, and soccer, but no baseball.

What would your typical 14-year-old do in this situation? My guess is that one might hear a lot of complaining, whining, yelling, and even crying. This is real-world stuff we are talking about. The absence of one's favorite activity, especially when expected, is really hard to accept.

Now enter Bryan Leib. Bryan isn't your typical anything. I've known Bryan for only about four years now, but this is a man who knows how to get shit done. Bryan, at the ripe age of 14, didn't complain about not having a team; he took action. He went to the head of the school and inquired about what he would need to accomplish to ensure baseball would be played for the next four years.

The head of the school gave him a very specific list and probably presumed Bryan wouldn't accomplish what was required. He didn't know who he was dealing with. The first requirement was for Bryan to collect 13 signatures from people in his class—sort of like a petition—agreeing baseball should be added as a varsity sport. Keep in mind there were only about 25 people in each class with approximately 12-13 of them boys. Bryan was able to collect 15 signatures as he wanted to exceed the 13 requested. He excitedly went to the head of the school to show off his success. The head of the school was duly impressed, and he and Bryan then had a more difficult conversation about funding. As Bryan now understands, but couldn't have possibly known then, varsity sports cost money—and oftentimes a lot of money. Coaches have salaries, uniforms aren't free, equipment is expensive, and, of course, there are logistics issues including buses, officials, and fields, which require an investment.

How much money was needed? The head of the school asked Bryan, a freshman, to find $5,000. If he was able to climb this seemingly monumental mountain, the head of the school would find a trustee to match the $5,000 and a baseball team would be formed. Now the challenge was on. How would a 14-year-old boy, desirous of forming a baseball team and not willing to take no as an answer, move forward? What would be his next move? He didn't realize it at the time, but he began to network. He began with the lowest-hanging fruit and those who were barely one degree of separation away from him. Two of his favorite people on the earth—his grandparents. Recognizing Bryan's passion, enthusiasm, and perseverance, his grandparents were in for $1,000. With one phone call, he was one-fifth of the way toward his goal.

When you are trying to get to yes, it's always easiest to start with those closest in your network. Pick off the low-hanging fruit and begin filling your basket. Gain confidence with a few answers of yes, because we all know there will be plenty of N-Os along the way. Little by little and piece by piece, Bryan got to his $5,000 goal. This is an amazing accomplishment for a 14-year-old with no track record and no real guarantee other than the word of the head of the school (which back then really meant something).

So Bryan rushed in to see his new business partner and showed him $5,000 in checks, and even some in cash. Showing the cash probably impressed the head of school even further as we all know what could potentially happen when you give a 14-year-old cash. Not, however, a focused and determined 14-year-old looking to succeed by building a varsity baseball team!!

And that is exactly what happened. Bryan succeeded and there was (and still is) a varsity baseball team at his high school. As you can imagine, they didn't have great success initially on the field. However, one could and should argue that getting to be on the field was the greatest success. After all, you can't win the game if you aren't in the game.

To me, Bryan Leib is the ultimate in grit, determination, and hustle. He knows what it takes to be a grinder. He is comfortable as both the chief lettuce picker-upper and the executive director of his organization appearing on local, regional, national, and international television as a spokesperson for topics around the Middle East. You see, Bryan learned at an early age that it takes hard work, a great attitude, and the ability to network to get what you want in life.

I met Bryan when he was running for Congress in Philadelphia's very important 3rd District. He was up against a formidable incumbent who had been part of the Philadelphia Democratic machine for decades and continues to be. The incumbent has served his constituency at the local, state, and now federal level, and his running as an incumbent Democrat is almost license for guaranteed victory in Philadelphia politics.

Enter Bryan and his dogged determination. I'd read about a Republican challenger to incumbent Dwight Evans and immediately thought to myself, *Who is this person and what is he thinking about?* A few weeks went by and I was at an event at the Museum of American

Jewish History, and as I was walking into the auditorium, Bryan came up to me and introduced himself as "Bryan Leib, candidate for the US House of Representatives, and I could use your help." At the time, I was working in the nonprofit sector and could not actively promote any candidates—although I was pulling for Bryan and hoping he could grab a rabbit out of the hat. Of course, he had longer odds than the 1969 New York Mets. But there was something about Bryan and I knew he'd put up a good fight.

He went into the neighborhoods, met with people, raised money from significant donors, stuck to his campaign pledge to bring much-needed change, and never took one day off. One could see his genuine care for what he was after. He was young and inexperienced but very authentic.

As predicted—it didn't take Nostradamus to make this call—Bryan lost. However, he garnered more than 20,000 votes. In my opinion, this was an incredible showing for a first-time candidate running on probably that same $10,000 budget he had as a freshman baseball player. If it was more, it wasn't a whole lot more!

I can't imagine what it would take to put your heart and soul into a political campaign and not be victorious. This process takes so much out of you physically, emotionally, and spiritually. However, all is not lost. The connections Bryan made, the speaking engagements, the fundraising and friend-raising, and all of the various activities it takes to run a campaign were all part of how Bryan continued to evolve.

Running his campaign was another get-shit-done moment. Have a goal and see it through regardless of the obstacles in front of you. Make phone calls, use your network, build your network, do what you say, and say what you do. These are all repeated themes in this handbook. This is really a simple strategy for reasonable success in life. But be genuine in your efforts and follow up with people on time and every time.

I asked Bryan about a mentor in his life and he mentioned two important people. The first, I never had the pleasure of meeting but wish I had. His maternal grandmother was a force in his life. She would be the first person he'd go to beaming with pride after any successful moment. Good grades in school, home run in baseball, new girlfriend—didn't matter. She was always the first and always the happiest, but she always kept him grounded.

"Okay," she would say after the hug and kiss. "So what's next?" This is such a great question. It's not that she didn't want him to revel in his success or enjoy the fruits of his labor. However, she wanted him to learn to build on that success. Take the momentum and keep going forward. She knew that if you aren't moving forward, you either aren't moving or are going in the wrong direction. She wanted him to think about what he had just done, what helped him to be a success, and what he could do to be even better the next time around. One thing is for sure, she was never interested in handing him a participation trophy.

The other mentor Bryan referred to is a very successful real estate entrepreneur from Philadelphia. This man is really a success in almost everything he does. He is still a reasonably young guy with a great story and his endorsement is critical if you want to be successful as an entrepreneur in the Philadelphia region. Bryan met him by chance.

Working as a development associate for a small nonprofit in Philadelphia, he was a given a list to follow up with. Basically cold call a bunch of strangers and ask for money. On the list of things that terrify people, I think this is right up there with the first guy that said yes to drinking milk after watching a farmer milk a cow!! But really, people don't like to call other people and ask them for money. A 2019 study showed that 48 percent of businesspeople hired to make sales calls have a phobia of calling others and asking them for money.

But not Bryan. He was hired to do a job and he had his list and he was going to get shit done. As he was making calls, he recognized the name of this gentleman and called him. He mentioned something to the effect that he knew this person and the organization had some issues in the past and he'd like to put that behind them and see if they could figure out a way to work together. Long story short, Bryan received a pledge for $5,000. But more importantly, a new relationship was formed. A mentor/mentee, big brother type of relationship. This person continues to play a major role in Bryan's development and Bryan doesn't make any major life decisions without first checking in

Not being afraid to pick up the phone and ask for the sale was key. Finding something the person could remember and relate to was factor number two—Bryan was immediately memorable. I wasn't on that call, but I am sure Bryan was authentic and humble as well.

In further discussion with Bryan, I asked him for advice for all of you out there. Bryan is now a very successful media contributor on many different channels. He even recently appeared on Saudi Arabia television talking about the Middle East geopolitical situation. Bryan spoke to me about being humble and working hard. Two critical factors I have always subscribed to.

Bryan shows us why finding your passion and working incredibly hard can be so fulfilling. Know that you are going to fall ten times, but you must continue to get up as failure is part of success (as we talked about earlier). Get up the eleventh time and that could be the most important time of all. People want to deal with those who are genuine and who fight for what is right. Display your passion and always be ready, willing, and able to raise the bar. Have frank and honest discussions but remember to always pick up the phone and make a phone call. You've read that countless times already. Don't ever discount the value of an old-fashioned phone call. Like the old catchphrase says, "Reach out and touch someone." Of course, they meant on the phone!!

If everyone had Bryan's drive, tenacity, spirit, enthusiasm, and desire, there would be many more successful and satisfied people in the world. He learned at a young age that if curiosity killed the cat, desire resuscitated it. Had I been a classmate of Bryan's when he was a freshman, I'd have been right beside him raising money, acquiring names, and helping to build that team. That lesson helped make Bryan who he is today. Bryan is still a young guy and I will put my money on his success over the next several years because he puts his money where his mouth is and puts others first.

CHAPTER EIGHT

Once You Get It, Take Care of It

Life is a journey that will offer you more bumps than thanks. How you respond to the bumps will define you much more than how you accept the thanks. Will you run and hide or will you stay and fight and learn and work harder? Sometimes the consequences are high, but there is always an alternative.

I moved from a spacious suburban neighborhood into Philadelphia's Center City in November 2019…just in time for the pandemic known as COVID-19. At the time, this seemed like a great idea. The ability to walk to work, restaurants, cultural attractions, and so much more. An entire city at your fingertips. Need something? It's a one-minute walk to pick it up. Big snowstorm coming? Who cares? Walk to work. Life was about to become so much easier and simpler.

But who could see COVID coming? Who knew what a pandemic and ensuing lockdown would do to a once-thriving metropolis? Factor in racial tension and a complete lack of leadership. You've all heard the saying "The emperor has no clothes." However, in our city, we created a new one: "The clothes have no emperor."

The once-crowded streets were lifeless. Stores once abuzz with activity had merchandise left in place for months, and the hospitality industry was crippled and left lifeless. I was never a fan of zombies and didn't understand anything about what a zombie apocalypse might look like, but one walk outside painted a picture for anyone who didn't know or understand. The streets were seemingly filled with vagrants, homeless, beggars, and hobos. I don't think these people weren't there before, but they had blended in with the tens of thousands of others who lined the streets daily. After all, when a city is crowded with businesspeople, leisure travelers, and others, it becomes electric, energetic, and mesmerizing in so many ways.

Now the streets were out of a movie. As I walked outside the only missing were the tumbleweeds. However, I began to really take note of not only the sheer number of people who were homeless but also who many of the regulars were. There was one gentleman who stood out to me. He seemed new to the homeless world, a bit cleaner and fresher, and he looked a lot more scared.

As I walked past him, he always made eye contact and I'd offer a hello. I don't give money to anyone who appears to be able-bodied and could be working. We were now in a pandemic, so I broke my rule and peeled off a dollar and handed it to him. I didn't really think much of the interaction. The next day I saw him again—same thing, but I had no cash so no dollar.

There were days I'd see him and days I wouldn't. Sometimes he'd be in the same location and others I'd find him in unexpected locations. I was going into my office now and again to check on the place. Since I was now within walking distance and in charge of the business, I felt the responsibility to be there.

Eventually I found out that this gentleman's name was Al and I began to greet him as "Whattup, Al?" That eventually got changed to Big Al as he was about six-foot-five. I was going to pick up lunch one day and decided to get him a sandwich too. I didn't ask him what he wanted as I presumed he'd be grateful for whatever I brought him. Plus, I like the element of surprise. No matter who you are dealing with in life, people like to be surprised—of course, when it's a good thing—as bad surprises can be really awful.

Al was not a particularly attractive character. In fact, he was hard to look at and I suspect even in his heyday, he'd have had a hard time meeting a woman in a female prison with a fistful of pardons. So when I handed him his sandwich, I was not particularly interested in dining with him. But I handed him his sandwich and a few PC condiments, a napkin, and a bottle of water. I remember the look on his face and might not ever forget it.

He took the package and thanked me. He looked sad and said, "I never imagined myself being homeless or living in the street." At this point, I had two moves: I could walk away and be a total dick. This is where I was leaning. Or, I could come up with some response and begin a conversation. Something inside me pushed in the don't-be-a-dick direction, and I replied with something like, "Oh, what happened?" I don't recall exactly what I said, but it was in that general direction.

Basically, I learned he had his own business, a family, friends, and owned his own home. He was living the American Dream. That dream is to be able to achieve success by working hard. Success can be defined in a variety of ways, but family, business, and homeownership are pretty solid metrics.

So of course I had to find out what happened. Big Al went on to tell me an incredible story of missteps, bad luck, tragedy, and unimaginably horrific timing. I mean if it weren't for bad luck, Big Al would have had none at all. The story was almost unimaginable. I don't want to give you the prince was born, he lived, he died version, but basically his wife died, and she had managed his bookkeeping. One of his children became ill and had to be hospitalized and his insurance didn't cover a lot of what was needed. It turned out his wife wasn't a great bookkeeper and he owed a lot of money, and he was going to have to sell his house. Oh, yeah, there was a second mortgage he didn't know about because there was a bad signature of his on the loan documents.

On and on and on. Was he making this up? I don't know. There was something about him that just seemed different. If you've ever seen the movie *Trading Places* with Eddie Murphy, Jamie Lee Curtis, and Dan Akroyd, you'll recall a scene where Dan Akroyd's character is trying to convince Jamie Lee Curtis's character that he isn't homeless. She asks to look at his hands and realizes they are soft and that he probably never worked a day in his life.

I didn't ask to hold Big Al's hands as I wasn't looking to touch him—especially during COVID-19 when I wasn't supposed to be touching anyone or anything and was busy scrubbing my box of graham crackers before they could come into the house. But something was different about this guy. His beard looked newer, his hair just a bit cleaner, and his clothes smelled a bit less.

Eventually I would go on to see Big Al in other locations and we'd have other conversations. I would periodically ask him follow-up questions and his story never wavered. He was able to recall details, dates, and locations.

What is the point of Big Al's story? Big Al seemingly did everything right. A college graduate and proprietor of his own business, he had a real life with a real family and a roof over his head. He had food on his plate and his future seemed not to be in question. Then after a series of unfortunate and unplanned events, it was all gone.

Life is precious and the things we work hard to acquire and accomplish are too. If you are going to take the time to build your network and build a career—regardless of what that career is—protect your investment. Consider it insurance. Never stop practicing your craft. Be a lifelong learner and continue to strive for greatness.

An old friend gave me two incredibly valuable pieces of advice when I was a young buck coming up in the grind. He said, "Steve—if you put your success in the hands of other people, you will fail every time." In some ways, this is depressing. Does it suggest you can't trust others? I never took it that way. I always took it to mean: If you want something, go get it. Don't let anyone stand in your way.

Take the bull by the horns and toss it to the ground if need be. The world is yours and you can be anything you want if you work hard and do all you can do.

It doesn't mean you can't or shouldn't work with others—just make sure you are in control. It's why I always stood up and volunteered to be a leader. Youth sports—I'm in. Board volunteer work—count on me. Someone needs a favor—call on me. Be there for others and be a role model. Working as hard as you can on things you love isn't work.

The other saying this same guy taught me was: "What they'll do *for* you, they'll do *to* you." A cautionary tale about how people are always going to look out for number one. It's perfectly fine to look out for number one—in fact, in the last paragraph, I encourage you to do just that. Always look out for number one—just don't step in number two (a Rodney Dangerfield joke). But while you are looking out for number one, just remember every other single person is doing the same thing.

Just be cautious of anyone who suggests breaking into the Pentagon to steal intel on your competitors. Might sound like a good idea because it may help you, but remember, those same folks will break into your house and rearrange your furniture when you aren't looking.

CHAPTER NINE

Can You See It?

The transformation for player to coach is not easy. What lessons did you learn as a player? How will you integrate your communication style and your coaching methods? Will you look to impart life lessons or just Xs and Os? There is a saying that the Jimmys and the Joes are more important than the Xs and the Os. Meaning, you have the players—what will you do with them?

Basketball has been an important part of my life for as long as I can remember. My first encounter with the game was in second grade, late by today's standards, but my family was a baseball family back in the day. I recall vividly being in gym class and our teacher having us do different drills during various weeks of the year—drills today's youth could benefit from. On one particular day, we had to stand under the basketball goal in the low block and attempt to make as many shots as possible in one minute.

I was probably seven years old at this point, and I was a giant—if not the tallest in the class, I was pretty close. I remember the whistle blowing, and at the end of the minute, I made either three or four baskets. It was humiliating as I just couldn't make a layup. The ball was always too high, too strong, and just too sloppy. I recall one of my best friends (still to this day) coming up to me after class and saying, "Man, you are the biggest kid in the class. You gotta make more shots than that." I knew we were going to be doing this drill again in a couple of weeks, and I would go to the park several days a week to practice. Eventually I ended up looking pretty good during the second try in gym class, making 15 shots in a minute. Still not great, but a vast improvement.

From that point on, I was consumed by basketball. I played in leagues, joined clinics, watched college and professional games, and truly enjoyed the magic the game possessed.

People who have played at exceptionally high levels or who have used the game for the betterment of themselves and others are an inspiration to me. In another life, there is no question I worked in the game in some capacity. Those who knew me growing up always heard me say I wanted to be the NBA commissioner. I had a job offer to work in the NBA back in 1987 but couldn't afford to live in New York City with the money the league offered at that time. I try not to think about what might have been, but… "With the first pick in the NBA Draft…"

I first met John "Jay" Timms in 2008, when he was the lead assistant basketball coach at The Friends Central School in Wynnewood, Pennsylvania—just beyond the Philadelphia city limits. The head coach of Friends Central was a friend of mine who was giving lessons to my oldest son, so I got to know Jay by spending time at Friends Central. FCS, as it is known by its student body, was a basketball powerhouse back in those days. That team in 2008 had a freshman named Amile Jefferson, who would go on to play at Duke University and for the NBA's Orlando Magic. The team started with five college players and had a great bench. It was one of the best high school teams I've seen and probably one of the best in the area throughout the past twenty years.

When you think of basketball in Philadelphia, there are no shortages of spectacular high school teams and players. This is like the heartbeat of high school hoops. Plenty of great high school ball has been played in Baltimore, DC, and, of course, New York City—but there's something special about the brand and style of Philadelphia hoops.

Jay had come from a great basketball background that included a short career at a Pennsylvania junior college where he was the all-time leading scorer and had an offer to play for Tubby Smith at the University of Georgia before an unfortunate incident had that taken away from him.

Despite that incident, because of which Jay learned the world is unfair and that a black man may not always be on the same equal footing as his white peers, he went on to a fantastic Division III career at Wilkes University, where he led the team to its two greatest seasons in school history. He also graduated with a 3.2 GPA as he knew that the education part of being in college was equally as important as the hardwood portion. However, at the conclusion of his career, there was no NBA Draft and overseas wasn't an option at that time.

So, Jay, being the smart person he is, saw an opportunity to open a small retail business in the heart of Wilkes-Barre, Pennsylvania. In the 1990s, this was not statistically the smartest route for him to take. In fact, naysayers discouraged him from opening his shop. However, like everything else that had come before in his life, he knew what he knew, and he was determined to make this business a success.

And a success he made it. The store was thriving, and Jay was content to be a businessman and was constantly seeking ways to make the business bigger and better. But one day, a friend told him about the Scranton Miners, an entrant in the Atlantic Basketball Association. He was now a few years past his playing days, but he decided to play for the Miners for a couple of games to see what it would be like. Of course, Jay scored thirty-plus points in each game, and he began to get the basketball itch again.

After a return trip to Philadelphia to train at Temple University with an Owls assistant coach and another coach, Jay suffered a stress fracture in his leg. However, he was still determined to make his comeback and seek an overseas opportunity. It was at this point that he sold his business for a handsome profit and became laser-focused on the game of basketball. He rehabbed the leg and continued training, playing, and practicing. He had found a basketball deal in Denmark that paid him a good salary, and he was excited to play basketball once again at a high level and in a professional league.

He joined one of Philadelphia's top men's leagues. This league featured players who today are playing in the NBA, but at that time, they were high school juniors and seniors. This was a high-profile and excellent league where the bar was going to be set high throughout every possession of every game. But it was exactly what Jay needed if he was going to go to Denmark in the best possible shape and at the top of his game. If he was going to Denmark, it was not to sit on the bench and play a few minutes a game. He was going to be a starter and play meaningful minutes and help contribute to a championship.

However, disaster struck once again. This time, Jay came down and he didn't have a stress fracture; he actually shattered his leg. If you recall the Paul George injury from several years ago, this was the same type of injury Jay experienced. Denmark wasn't just on hold; it was over. Basketball was not in the cards—he was just hopeful that walking normally would be an option after that. One of the first words Jay heard from the doctor was "amputation." If you know Jay the way I know Jay, you understand, this man only knows one way, and that way is forward. He sets a goal and meets that goal. He knows what he wants, and he works hard to go get it. So when the doctor mentioned that word, Jay knew he'd have whatever surgeries were needed, and while he might not be able to play professionally, he was going to play at some level again.

Sure enough, Jay stands in front of us today with both of his legs. While grafting and other procedures were needed, making it difficult for him to perform certain daily activities like extending his arm fully, if you were to look at him on any given day, you would not only not notice anything out of the ordinary, but you would also begin to hum the tune "Sharp Dressed Man" by ZZ Top.

At this point, Jay knew that retail wasn't his calling. After a two-year hiatus from the game that included not playing, watching, or even talking much about hoops, he realized he needed the game of basketball and wanted to be part of it, but now as a coach. He desired to impart his knowledge, energy, and wisdom to the next generation of talented Philadelphia players. The players continued to evolve, growing bigger, stronger, and faster. The swag and the gear become more important and far more expensive, but one thing remains a constant…young players need good mentors and coaches to help guide them. To keep them from coloring too far outside the lines and to keep them and their goals focused. It doesn't always work out, but Jay was going to do everything he could to help lead the way.

He began his coaching career at a local Philadelphia public high school and eventually found his way to a charter high school, helping to form a league of charter schools. At the time, he realized charter schools had an advantage regarding young players in Philadelphia. At that time, neither the Philadelphia Public League nor the Catholic League participated in the PIAA State Championship. Once the Pub and Catholic League Champions were crowned, they would play each other to determine who was the best in the city, and that would end the season. There are many seasons where the best team in Philadelphia was no doubt the best team in the Commonwealth of Pennsylvania. But if the games are not played, it's only hyperbole.

But Jay, being the smart man he is, saw that the charter schools were eligible for the state tournament and that this could give him an edge, helping him to lure some of the better players to play for him. He, along with two other very notable coaches, were leaders in the charter basketball movement that now dominates the Pennsylvania State Tournament at every division—from A to AAAAAA every year. Now, both the Public League and Catholic League participate in States, so most years, the champion does indeed come from District 12 of the PIAA.

All of this came prior to him going to coach at the Friends Central School, where we met. He was well-known throughout the basketball community, and he was not only a great coach but a mentor and a leader to the young people who played for him.

He was going to be the mentor that he never had. Jay is proud to say he had "people who showed me what not to do." Perhaps he was an early adopter of the saying "It takes a village…," and/or he was the beneficiary of having people in his life who recognized he had greatness in him and wanted to ensure the best possible road to success for Jay.

Most of us have greatness in us, but it takes hard work, dedication, perseverance, and determination to get us to realize whatever our potential is. Far too many people don't reach that potential or even begin to scratch the surface. It's much easier to take the short road, the shortcut, and it's certainly easier to leap over short objects. But greatness takes more than the short road. Jay saw that, and more importantly, he had others pulling him away if he appeared to be headed in the wrong direction.

In 2013, Jay saw an opportunity. His son was playing football with a group of young men who didn't have an opportunity to also play basketball. His son was developing into a very good player, and he realized that there are many young people out there who don't have the same opportunities as his own son. Because he had access to a gym, he could make time available to these young men on days when they didn't have football practice.

Little did he or anyone else know, this would be the beginning of the John Jay All-Stars. This group of football-first young men would go on to play in and win tournaments. But first and foremost, they were learning great life lessons about being on the court and what it meant to be a great teammate.

While Jay's program has evolved and grown, it continues to teach young men about basketball while developing them as young men and productive citizens. Jay focuses on several core philosophies, and winning basketball games is not the first priority. Jay could have made a deal to coach in a bigger, more established program, but he wanted to coach his style using his philosophy.

One of the first things he teaches these young men is to always exert maximum effort. This is important both on and off the court. Putting in maximum effort not only shows respect but also allows others to say, "You did your best." Whatever the results are, nobody can take away the fact that you did your best. Keep in mind that sometimes maximum effort isn't enough. Sometimes the other team, player, or person is just better than you. In a game like basketball, you may very well be giving your all, but in most scenarios, so is your opponent. Someone's maximum effort will outlast the other.

Another lesson Jay teaches is "good before fancy." Again, he relays real-life examples and not basketball. While in hoops, the traditional bounce pass is probably a safer bet than the behind-the-back pass, but it's the latter that will get the crowd out of its seats and maybe put you in the news highlights. However, too many behind-the-back passes will also lead to turnovers and easy baskets for the other team.

In life, if you want to buy a fancy car but can't afford insurance and gas, what is the purpose of having a fancy car? Live within your means. Sure, four girlfriends might sound great, but one girlfriend is all you need. Less is oftentimes more, and while fancy might be sexy, good is usually steady. Let's not forget the story of the tortoise and the hare. The hare goes off as the heavy favorite—he's younger, faster, stronger, and a shoo-in to win a race against the methodical old tortoise. But the hare doesn't pace himself, and he's not careful. He takes too many risks, and at the end of the race, he's on the sidelines, clutching and grabbing because he doesn't have the energy to finish when the tortoise passes him. The tortoise was good; the hare was fancy. There are people in history who have had the unique ability to be both good and fancy at the same time. In basketball, Magic

Johnson, Larry Bird, and the Harlem Globetrotters all come to mind. There are artists like Lady Gaga or Nicki Minaj that fall into that category. But generally speaking, if you subscribe to the theory of "good before fancy," you are going to have a lot more success in your life than failure.

Once you do achieve some success, learn the difference between fans and supporters. If you achieve a certain level of success on the court, your fans are going to cheer when you put the ball in the hoop, and they may boo you if you don't succeed. That isn't support—it's fandom. Being a fan is great, and it is every person's right—but being your fan doesn't mean someone is your supporter. Your supporters are your people—your ride-or-die crew. You miss a free throw at the end of the game that could have put your team into overtime, your supporters are still there waiting for you at the end. Your fans are in their cars, cursing you out. Your people are with you win or lose, succeed or fail, high or low.

We all need supporters every day. We don't need fans. Social media has made us all crave fans—we seek likes, thumbs-ups, comments, smiles, hearts, or any type of validation of what we do. We don't *need* that; we *desire* that. We need supporters to get us through the tough times, to help us enjoy the good times, and to be there through the mundane, everyday times.

Lastly, as Jay is teaching, coaching, counseling, mentoring, or just being a friend, you will hear him ask, "Can you see it?" He's asking if you understand. If you can, you see and feel what he is talking about. If you can visualize it, you can do it. He could be talking about making the perfect bounce pass, or he could be talking about how to speak to one of your teachers. But walk into a gym where Jay is conducting a clinic or practice and be prepared to hear, "Can you see it?" Next time you are learning something or hearing something for the first time, think about if you can see it. Because if you can see it, you can be it.

The world needs more people like Jay Timms. It takes a lot of hard work and determination, but we all have an inner Jay Timms. The coach, counselor, mentor, leader, friend, buddy, role model, or father figure. We can do it. We can all pay it forward like Jay does. We need to take the extra step and see how we can do it and where. The recipe is easy…one part maximum effort, one part good before fancy, one part knowing who your supporters are, and one part knowing what not to do.

Can you see it?

CHAPTER TEN

The Underdog

The common theme in this book is overcoming adversity and using your network to help you push forward. Most of us are underdogs, or at least it appears that way. We have had to work hard, study harder, find opportunities, and deal with rejection. How the underdog goes through life is much different than the favorite or the superstar. How will the underdog set itself apart?

In another chapter, we touched on the tortoise and his ascent to victory over the heavily favored hare in a race for the ages. When Aesop, the Greek fabulist and storyteller, created this tale about the tortoise and the hare, it is unlikely he was foreshadowing an outcome of good vs. evil or even a classic underdog story. We may never truly know what Aesop was telling us, so it is up to us to interpret. This tale has been told many times and in many ways over the decades.

My version is simple as I will explain. A heavy favorite was upset at the finish by a competitor nobody thought had a chance. This is a story we've seen repeated in television, movies, scripture, and in own our lives time and again. It's why, when we wager on a game, it's called "gambling." There are no sure things, no predicted certainty in outcomes—it's why they play the games.

When we consider some of the other great underdogs that we have come across, there are many names of both individuals and teams to consider. Rocky Balboa; Rudy Ruettiger; the team from Marion, Indiana, portrayed in the movie *Hoosiers*; Buster Douglas;

Wilma Rudolph; David when he slayed Goliath; and, of course, the greatest underdog story of our lives—the 1980 United States Men's Olympic Hockey Team. Where the chant "U-S-A" began. Where the unthinkable and the unimaginable happened. Where the words "Do you believe in miracles…? Yes!" became part of our lore, and where mere mortals became legends instantly.

What is the common trait of these considerable underdogs? Since I have not studied each as a psychologist might, I can only surmise that grit, determination, hard work, and the ability to rise after each fall are the first places to look.

I added the fictional character Rocky Balboa to this list just to add emphasis. Not only was *Rocky* a classic underdog story, but Sylvester Stallone in 1976 was too. He was not the megastar he is today, and this movie was not expected to do well, let alone win an Academy Award. Stallone had been a struggling actor and was even working outside of Hollywood just to make a living. But he had an idea for a screenplay and a vision to portray down-on-his-luck Balboa in the film himself, even though there was talk of talented and experienced actors like Burt Reynolds or Robert Redford playing the protagonist. Stallone forged ahead, and we all know that the rest is history.

Stallone was vigilant in his networking and his follow-up. He was determined to make his career a success, and he knew he had a winning idea with his screenplay *Rocky*. It was up to him to make it a success. He used all of his tools and zigged when others might have zagged, went high when others could have gone low, and most importantly, like the character he played in the movie, he got up off the canvas every single time he was knocked down. He understood that success without failure is not possible. Tenacity, hard work, and determination can often overcome failure.

When you consider, in my opinion, the greatest sports story of the last one hundred years—or maybe ever—it's hard not to think of the events involving the 1980 United States Olympics as the ultimate underdog story. The movie that covers this story is even called *Miracle*. If you were alive when this event took place, you'll recall vividly where you were when the USA defeated the mighty Soviet Red Army. The same Soviet team who toured the NHL over the years and dismantled professional teams. This Soviet team was as close to a sure thing as there was ever going to be in sports.

Since legalized sports gambling wasn't even a thing in 1980, outside of Nevada, my guess is the odds for the Soviets to win the gold medal were probably even money. A staggering favorite with almost no close second. As for the Americans, they were a team of amateurs from great hockey schools like the University of Minnesota and Boston University. This was before professionals were allowed to play for the USA.

This team was given no shot at even a bronze medal. Offering serious competition for the gold was as unlikely as winning a $600 million Powerball. Once the team was selected, Coach Herb Brooks was relentless with them in their training and practice. If nothing else, they were going to outwork and outhustle their opponent. They'd be in the best shape of their lives, and exhaustion would not be a reason they might lose. Physical and mental preparation were critical keys for Coach Brooks. He was doing everything and anything to get them to work and think as a cohesive and well-orchestrated group. Knowing that the sum of the parts is greater than any one piece, a team clicking on all cylinders, working as hard and smart as possible, could be a success. But what did success look like against a team like the Soviets? For Coach Brooks, winning a gold medal would be a success.

After playing an exhaustive pre-Olympic exhibition schedule, the team's final game was against the powerful Soviets in Madison Square Garden. After months and months of training, Coach Brooks and his staff would get an opportunity to see where his team stood against the mighty Red Army. When the game was over, it was hard to look at the scoreboard. The Soviets had scored ten goals—ten. In hockey, that is a massive number. The upstart USA team could muster only three, and they were fortunate to get that many. The score wasn't even as close as the numbers were on the scoreboard. With the Olympic Games about to start in Lake Placid, there was very little left for the coaching staff to say or do other than hope and pray.

The rest is history. The team had good success throughout the round-robin portion of the event, and they gained confidence. This is so important in your climb to success. Take one step at a time, don't trip, and keep going up. Try to take three steps at once, and you might slip or fall. If some confidence is good, more is better. Eventually they got to the medal round, and who did they find on the opposite end of the ice? The Soviet Red Army. The team that just a few weeks earlier had put a hurtin' on them so bad that they all questioned whether they belonged. Now they had defied most odds and were playing for the right to compete for the gold medal.

As the team was preparing to take the ice and waiting inside their locker room, in came Coach Brooks. He was focused on one thing and one thing only—winning. He and his staff had done everything possible to prepare the team for this moment. But had they done enough? Did his team truly believe they had what it took to win this game?

At the time, the Soviets and the United States were mortal enemies, still locked in the Cold War. Just months earlier, the Soviet Union had invaded Afghanistan, causing a ripple effect across the world. The world didn't know what was going to come next, and here stood the Soviet Red Army hockey team—perhaps the most invincible sports team ever assembled—ready to once again face off with the United States Olympic hockey team. So what did Coach Brooks have up his sleeve? What words of wisdom might he have conjured up?

Well, he said this: "Great moments are born from great opportunity, and that's what you have here tonight, boys. That's what you've earned here tonight. One game; if we played them ten times, they might win nine. But not this game, not tonight."

Now they had to go out onto the ice and take advantage of this once-in-a-lifetime opportunity. They came out hard. At the end of the first period, the game was tied at 2-2. This gave Team USA incredible confidence. They were right there with only two periods left—two long periods—but they were in the game. In the next period, the Soviets took a one-goal lead and, heading into the final session, the Soviets led 3-2. While they were down, and the hill seemed like a mountain, it was a far cry from 10-3. On this day, as Coach Brooks opined, his team was the equal of the Soviets. In the critical third period, the USA team tied the score on a power play goal by Mark Johnson. That was quickly followed by another goal by team captain Mike Eruzione, who gave the USA the lead with exactly ten minutes to go. How would the United States respond now, with the crowd in a frenzy and during what would feel like the longest ten minutes of everyone's lives?

Because of broadcast rules back in 1980, the game was not shown live. It would be shown later that evening on what was referred to as tape delay. I remember watching the local news and the sports came on. The reporter said, "We are about to show the score of the hockey game played between the United States and the Soviet Union—look away if you don't want to know." This was before social media, and I went into the game that evening not knowing who had won or what had happened. That was the real miracle!!

Well, needless to say, the United States team relied on its grit and determination. All those hours and hours of practice and muscle memory. Their inability to grow fatigued mentally or physically. Their team concept and the reliance on their goaltender, Jim Craig, who stopped shot after shot. It seemed like the Soviets were firing shots from a cannon, but none passed Jim Craig, who played the game of his life. "Great moments are born from great opportunities..." This is true in all of our lives each and every day. A gold medal isn't always on the line. Sometimes a deadline for a project is forthcoming or some special birthday or anniversary; whatever you are about to face, will you rise up, or will you fall down?

Preparedness and preparation, combined with confidence and know-how, is a great recipe for success that we must all learn. Mixing these ingredients will typically end with some positive result in your life. Think about anything and everything you've ever wanted to do or tried to do. If you've not practiced or are trying something for the first time, there is a good probability you won't be that good at what you are doing. However, if you are prepared, have practiced, and exude confidence, I'd put my money on you almost every time. Sure, there are exceptions to this rule, but if you rely on the network you've built, and you work in a manner that makes you comfortable, you will succeed. Remember what Jay Timms said—good before fancy.

So the USA beat the Red Army in what *Sports Illustrated* called the greatest game of the twentieth century. What most people don't think about is that the USA still had one more game to play to win the gold. They faced a very good Finland team. How would the USA respond after the biggest victory they could hope for? Would a silver medal be good enough? Was victory over the Red Army all they needed to come out as heroes? Or would losing in the gold medal game erase that incredible and unforgettable accomplishment?

The United States was losing 2-1 heading into the third and final period. I know I didn't have a good feeling. I wasn't in the locker room but was hopeful Coach Brooks had another great motivational speech for them. This time, he looked at them stoically and said, "If you lose this game, you will take it to your fu**ing graves." He then walked out, and as he did, he turned back over his shoulder and repeated, "Your fu**ing graves!" I guess that was enough because they reached down and scored three more times for a 4-2 gold medal victory, lifting a nation into a frenzy that is unimaginable today.

So to be an underdog doesn't mean victory is not possible. It simply means the work is harder, the hill steeper, and perhaps the journey longer. But success will always taste sweeter. In today's sports landscape, many athletes are vilified for leaving one team to join another and create what is known as a super team. Some fans become upset because they see a great player taking a perceived easy route to success and a championship. Most regular people live in a day-to-day grind. We are hustlers, and the journey is what makes things so interesting to us. When we see someone taking what we perceive to be the easy way out, it's disturbing on many levels.

There are no free lunches in life as an adult. The streets are paved with bumps and ditches. Most people don't win the lottery and get to sail off into the sunset. We work hard, pay our bills, try to enjoy the time we aren't working, and then start all over again.

The underdog story is the great American story. The United States of America is an underdog story itself. It has grown to become the greatest nation in the history of the planet. That is indisputable. You may not like certain things, but each and every day, hundreds of thousands of people do whatever they can to make their way here. The signers of the Declaration of Independence are some of the greatest thinkers ever. They are far from perfect humans as they lived in a time when there were many wrongs in society. But they created an idea in the Constitution, and it's stood the test of time. It's been our guidepost for more than 230 years.

So if our nation is an underdog, it only makes sense that we gravitate to stories of the less fortunate, the unexpected, the surprises. Where were you when Buster Douglas knocked out the invincible Mike Tyson? What would you have said if you'd been on the finish line watching the tortoise cross before the hare? If you had been there when David slayed the nine-foot giant Goliath with a perfect shot between the eyes, what would you have thought? You'd have probably said, "That could have been me. That should have been me. That will be me."

With a little luck and a lot of practice, you can do it. You are the ultimate underdog in a sea of underdogs. Never underestimate your opponent. Always sprint through the finish line and keep your head held high. You got this.

CHAPTER ELEVEN

Put Me In, Coach

No matter what your position is in life, know where you stand at any given moment. What is your role and what are the roles of those around you? This doesn't mean you can't or shouldn't color outside the lines of what you are supposed to do, but in order to do so you have to understand the expectations first.

No matter what the world is like at any given moment, youth sports thrive. The implosion of financial markets, international conflicts abroad, or domestic unrest… It doesn't matter. Parents continue to enroll their children in youth sports activities at incredibly high rates. This recession-proof phenomenon is what I refer to as "The Funnel." Think of a funnel—so much goes in at the top, yet so little comes out at the bottom.

Why do I refer to this as a funnel? A plurality of parents enrolls their children in sports (and other activities) as a possible means to an end. Maybe their son or daughter will become a great high school athlete who garners a college scholarship of some type. Dare we even dream about playing beyond high school? Damn the statistics and probability scale of any of this happening—we know we have the formula to be the next Richard Williams or Earl Woods.

The eagerness with which kids are signed up for sports is staggering. Organized sports begin as early as four years old, and I've read about soccer leagues for three-year-olds. We need to start them early so they don't miss out, so they can get an edge. Then we have to figure out training and special private coaching. How do we get our child noticed? How do we make him/her better, stronger, faster?

So the funnel syndrome is really due to the fact that at an early age everyone has potential, interest, and desire. Practices, training, lessons. The excitement and energy are boundless at the top of the funnel. But the years go by, and practices get longer, the games get in the way of other activities and interests, and some young people aren't as good as they used to be. Some were never any good, and at seven years old, it didn't matter, but at eleven, it does. So little by little, kid by kid, they fall out. By the time they are in junior high school, the funnel is squeezing out just a few players. There aren't many left. What happened to them all? Where did they go? What are they doing now? Well, they found other interests—things they enjoyed more, were better at, or just weren't nearly as bad at doing.

It's really quite interesting, and to me, it has become synonymous with life in general. It's easy to find something you like early. Things seem interesting and exciting, and you want to participate. But then you realize it's a bit more of a grind than you first anticipated. Those fun practice sessions have become laborious. So what do you do? How do you get from the excitement stage and blow past the burnout stage? It's really different for everyone, but you have to understand your own place and desires. What do you want out of whatever you have decided to do? Do you want to be a high school athlete or a high school athletic star? Do you want to go on and play in college? When you get that first job, do you want to grow with the company and become a senior executive or maybe even the president of the company? The lessons learned through participation in sports are often more important than learning the sport itself.

Whenever you submerse yourself in an activity, you want to become as good as you can possibly be in that activity. However, the uniform eventually does come off permanently for everyone. For the majority of participants, that age is around twelve years old. After your first organized participation, if you don't excel or have a whole lot of fun, you probably are opting for a different activity.

Most kids don't have the desire, drive, or staying power to become Michael Jordan. Jordan was cut from teams until midway through his high school career. Can you imagine the coaches who didn't think MJ was good enough? But at that moment in time, he wasn't. Many young people with lesser mindsets would have given up and found another activity. But not Michael. He not only pushed through, he also knocked down every barrier there was and became the greatest player of all time. But so many are simply satisfied with either good enough or happy to have tried.

This is why lessons learned, friendships made, and learning to both win gracefully and lose with pride are so critically important. Nobody likes a bad winner or sore loser. As we talked about earlier, if you put forth your best effort and come up short, there is nothing to be sorry for or to look down upon. Not everyone can win, and certainly not everyone can be the best. Life doesn't work that way. Some people own businesses, and others work as employees. No matter where you are in the hierarchy, the only thing that matters is hard work and showing up to do your absolute best. Hopefully, lessons like this were taught to you early in life and perhaps on a ballfield someplace.

After being involved in youth sports as a volunteer administrator for close to two decades, I heard every excuse, analogy, idea, and criticism there was to be heard. I saw bad parents, bad coaches, good parents and good coaches, bad administrators and good ones. Somewhere along the way, this became more business than fun, and the idea of who the customer was became blurred.

One minute, ABC's *Wide World of Sports* was showing the final Little League World Series championship game, and the next, the entire tournament was on television for several weeks. Games began well into the evening and were televised on a national cable sports network. Games played by eleven- and twelve-year-olds were seen as significant content. There are actually betting lines and money-line favorites on the outcome of each game. Is it a matter of time before NIL deals become available to Little Leaguers? Corporate America is trying to cash in, and Little League, with its "We don't pay our volunteers" mantra, is still raking in a lot of money from television rights and novelty and concession revenue, as well as rights fees from the network.

Sure, they don't pay the coaches or the umpires, but they certainly capitalize on the free market economy, so why shouldn't the kids?

The world has a "get yours" and a "get mine" feel to it. A rush to finish, to get in line and not be able to sit and enjoy the moment. Coaching your child is a gift, and so many of us screw this up. We are too obnoxious, too loud, too ornery, or just too wrapped up in ourselves to remember that these are young kids looking to have fun, learn a new game, and try to make friends.

Don't let your new job, new career, or new location get in the way of any of this. Look upon each new step as a new season. Trying on the new uniform or getting new shoes/cleats/pads, whatever you are doing should be embraced with unbridled enthusiasm for the beginning of the season. Beginnings are just that—new, fresh, starting points where hopefully the score is zero to zero. The playing field may not always be fair or equal, but as long as there is an opportunity to win, go out and play.

We talked earlier about winning and the importance of coming out on top. The reality is, not everyone will win—that's an impossible situation. However, as long as you have a chance to win, as long as the field is not predetermined, go out and give it your all. Leave no stone unturned and kick through barriers. Listen to your coaches and those looking to help you along the way.

The playing time might not always be equal, and life isn't a team activity. You have to rely on others and utilize assistance when and where it comes. The wide receiver has a hard time scoring if the quarterback doesn't either pass him the ball or call an end-around running play. The center in basketball may not be able to score if not in position to receive a great pass from the lead guard.

It's a journey; go out and enjoy it and participate in it as robustly as possible. If you want to be in the game, put yourself in. You don't have to sit on the bench asking to be put in. "Put me in, coach" should be something you are begging for him to do, not hoping he'll do. Kids today have a code for when things get exciting—LFG. So wake up and do it. Nike has one of the greatest slogans ever created: Just Do It. Live your life that way each and every day.

CHAPTER TWELVE

This Is What I Do

We get knocked down in life—sometimes it feels like a daily occurrence. There is always someone who has it worse than we do, but our problems are still our problems. Dealing with incredible adversity and overcoming long odds isn't easy. When the world counts you out—or worse, stops counting you completely—what will you do to get back in the game?

I've always been a fan of boxing. The "sweet science" as it is called. Why the sweet science? Because boxers must be both fierce and tactical while anticipating their opponent's next move. I never actually climbed into the ring for a real fight, but I have had occasions to spar a couple of times. Most importantly, I've used boxing as a training method. Boxers are some of the most well-trained and in-shape athletes on the planet. If you have ever tried to throw punches while moving for several three-minute periods, you know what I mean. For a number of years, I hadn't done much boxing or training and found myself longing to get back to pounding pads, throwing a hook-jab combination, and really working off a good sweat.

I wasn't looking to join a gym and take one of those fake boxing classes that really is a lot of dancing and jumping but not a whole lot of punching and technique. Then one day, about six years ago, a friend of mine from the way-back machine, who, like me, had moved from the western part of Pennsylvania to the southeastern portion, called me to tell me about a new boxing trainer he'd recently met. They had met at a Dunkin' Donuts as both were carrying boxing bags, and next thing you know, I had myself a new boxing trainer. However, this gentleman turned out to be a whole lot more than just a trainer. Ultimately, he became like family to me, and his journey in life has been very different than most people's. This guy was both a literal and figurative fighter.

During my first call with Michael Cerminaro, I knew I'd just been introduced to a guy who I'd be talking to regularly. Our conversation lasted more than an hour, and I learned more about him than I had anticipated. In addition to boxing, I was already sold on his masonry skills, and he had a really incredible outlook on life. He'd come up the hard way and spent time in places most of us can't even think about in our worst nightmares. He'd slept in places and done things that maybe you see in movies, but mostly you read about in bad fiction. He had a hard life and was finally coming up aces, and I found him interesting, fascinating, and, most of all, completely, authentically real. Not an easy characteristic to find in some people.

Ironically, I was also in need of a stone mason to do some major work on our front porch, which was sinking faster than the *Titanic*. So we set up a meeting. He was going to come to my house and do two things. First, give me an estimate on the much-needed repairs to the front walk, and second, join me in pounding pads for an hour or so. I was excited to meet my new friend, Mikey Mitts. Mitts, as most people called him, started using that name while he was working as an enforcer for a group of people who loaned money and needed muscle for collection—and the name Mikey Mitts, or Mitts, just caught on.

In that first hour, I knew Mitts had come from a serious problem with drugs and that he had overcome it. It is a constant battle and truly the ultimate fight. As Mitts said to me, "Climbing into the ring is easy—even if you get your ass kicked." He then went on, "The drug habit is the real fight."

The day Mitts was supposed to show up, I called him in the morning to confirm, and the first time, there was no answer. Then I called again, and a stranger picked up, saying, "Ain't no Mitts here." I began to worry, so I called our mutual friend. It turned out that Mitts had disappeared. This was not the first time this had happened. He had found an old friend and went on a bender and was missing. Because I have connections and a vast network, I called friends of mine in the Philadelphia Police Department, but to no avail. There was little to nothing they could do since I was technically not able to file a missing person's report, and nobody else was there to do so.

So I presumed the worst and was disappointed. Not because my steps wouldn't be repaired or because I wasn't going to get a good training session in, but because here was a guy who was trying to turn it all around but had hit a bad spot and was now probably somebody I'd never see again.

So basically, I forgot about him as months went by and I heard nothing. Every once in a while, I'd ask our mutual friend who had no real update. Then out of the blue, I got a call from a number I didn't know, and there was Mitts. He told me his story and apologized, and I was now even more determined to meet him. What he went through and survived is remarkable. I told him he owed me no apology and that I was happy to begin again. Unfortunately, I couldn't wait on the stonework and that was now complete, but I was very interested in the boxing training.

We finally met in Rittenhouse Square in Center City, Philadelphia, and we had a great lesson. We didn't have a lot of time to talk as he had client after client as this was now his main source of income. He was looking to build a boxing gym and training center. He was really good and was working with a family member. This went on for a couple of years—we had a lot of lessons, and I introduced him to a number of my friends who were seeking alternative workouts.

Eventually this led to him working out with different people on the beach at the Jersey Shore. He'd begin around 8:00 a.m. and go all morning. These were great day trips as he brought his then-girlfriend and her kids, whom he treated better than most people treat their own children.

Mitts continued to struggle, however, with addiction, and there were times when he'd disappear. I'd call his people and would go looking for him myself. I met a number of people in the Mitts web of contacts. You see, even when you are not in the traditional suit-and-tie business world, you need contacts in the world. Networking is never far away.

I remember one day, I walked into the barbershop Mitts had told me he hung out in. I met Joey the Barber. I walked in with my shirt and tie, and Joey looked at me and figured I was either a cop or I was lost. Not a lot of suits walking in to see Joey the Barber. Once I told him why I was there, he hugged me and thanked me. I spent the next several hours in that area with Mitts's picture, looking in places most people don't even know exist. I was texting with his girlfriend the entire time, and she knew I had about as much shot at finding him as did winning the Powerball, but I was determined.

Finally, I gave up and I reached out to some other folks I knew from down the way, and I circulated his picture. Eventually Mitts returned like he always did. I think he expected me to be either mad at him or disappointed in him. I was neither. I don't begin to pretend to understand what demons he was fighting, but I know he was at a point where he needed friends. It's like when Paulie looked at Rocky and said, "Friends don't owe. They do because they wanna do." It's like that. It's why you have friends, contacts, and relationships. So that when you are in that situation where you need help or must text 9-1-1 to someone, you know that someone is going to be there. The person you call and ask, "Where are you?" And the answer is always, "Turning around to come see you."

About a year or so later, Mitts found himself in a place most people fear—he was back in lockup. I went to visit with him one December morning, and we chatted. I looked into his eyes and could see a man who was focused on getting back and climbing the mountain. Fear was not an emotion that he had. At least, not in the way you might. His fear was of returning to where he sat at that moment. Fear of not succeeding and fear of letting his family down…again. He was too smart and too talented to be sitting there. He had a problem, and he had to address it head-on, and he was ready for that challenge. I was incredibly inspired by him that day, and I knew that he was going to pick himself up, dust himself off, and start all over again.

I think you get the background with Mitts. Eventually he married his then-girlfriend and adopted both kids. He's an incredible father and husband and is always there. Soon after he was released, he began working as a stone mason for a guy who looked him in the eye and said, "You are only worth $18 an hour, so that is all you are getting paid." That was the wrong thing to say to Mitts.… A man does not and should not tell another man what he's worth. But Mitts needed the work, and he swallowed his pride again and took the job. He was back into the boxing training world too. He'd wake up early in the morning—by 4:00 a.m.—and wouldn't finish until 10 or 11:00 p.m., and then he'd wake up and do it all over again.

Finally, his wife suggested he try to grab a side hustle and do some stonework himself. He bought an ad on social media, and that was that. He immediately began getting call after call, and within weeks, Cerminaro and Sons was born. He was his own boss and was off and running. His wife joined him on one of his first jobs, a stucco repair in an old-style basement. It was a monster of a job, and she didn't even know where he'd begin. He had a long weekend ahead of him, and she turned to him and asked, "What are you even going to do with this?" He looked at her with amazing confidence and said, "This is what I do!" And that is what he did. Finished the job on time and on budget.

He was now officially the most intense grinder I knew. Up at 3:00 a.m. and out in the field until at least 10:00 p.m. every day, seven days a week. Bidding jobs, meeting clients, finding the best deal on flagstone and other supplies, and continuing to get a leg up on his competitors.

Mitts knows what is on the other side. He knows what failure looks like, and he fully understands what success looks like. He also came to understand that success can be equally scary—in a far better way, of course. But now, his fears lie in those who depend on him. His wife, his two kids, his mom, and others he takes care of. He had the ultimate transformation—he went from existing to living. He relishes every minute of every day.

He's out hustling, meeting new clients, networking, following up, taking care of his employees, and being the best person he knows how to be.

You've heard from others about their approach to meeting people and how they network and build their connections. Mitts is the kind of person who easily knows how to read a person. He sums people up into one of three categories right away so he can determine how to follow up with them or if he should at all.

The first group is the "Hi and Bye" group. Some people are going to look you up and down and give you a quick (and sometimes empty) greeting. You know right away this person is not a stop-and-talk person. Hi and Bye—be nice and say hello and so long but move along as there is not much to see here. They may call if they need something, but you won't hear much from them.

The next group is the Distancers. This is the group that you don't even want to be in the Hi/Bye situation with. You meet them and you know they aren't for you—Hi and Bye is too much conversation. Bad luck or bad news comes along with this group, and it's time to move along. And, like the great Satchel Paige once said, "Don't look back."

The Thorough Stock Set is the final group. These are the people you know you want to have in your life. The people you can count on, the folks that will be there for you no matter what the circumstances. This is your ride-or-die crew. You meet them at various times and for various reasons and often unexpectantly. But there they are, and you are grateful they are in your life.

Mitts is proud that he has five people in his life he can call great friends, and I'm honored to be on his list, along with Joey the Barber. When you can impact someone in this manner, it really carries through in your own life in a meaningful way—a way that perhaps you didn't expect or think possible.

He lives by an important code. There is no BIG I or LITTLE U. If you feel like a little you when you are around a certain person, start spending time with other people. Look inside and decide whether it is really the other person or whether you are partly responsible for how you are feeling at that moment. As one of my son's coaches would say, "In this world, there is only one thing we can control, and that's our attitude." He always had them break huddle with ATTITUDE. Then one day, one of the players said, "Coach, you know there is one other thing you can control." Coach asked, "What's that?" The player replied, "Your body odor." BODY ODOR didn't seem like a positive huddle break, but the point was well-taken. So if you control your attitude, maybe the little you can turn into a big F YOU to the person whom you have an issue with. That is what Mitts will tell you.

Today, Mitts has a thriving stone installation business, two wholesale stone yards, a rental property, a beautiful home, and a great family, and is surrounded by people he loves. He is a great boss who treats his employees like he wanted to be treated when he was an employee, and now when I call him and he doesn't answer, I know he's just busy. He's not off the rails on a bender someplace. I told him that is the best compliment I can pay him. He went from being on my list of people to worry about to my list of people not to worry about. He found a solid core in his wife, who has been his rock. She has never wavered from his side, and they have an incredible family.

Mitts has shown that networking comes in all shapes and sizes. It comes in all styles and forms, and it never stops. If you hit rock bottom, you better have a good network to call upon to help raise you back up. If you are on top, you better not forget the little people who helped get you there.

This smart young man who started his business out of the back of a Nissan Altima and some borrowed masonry tools has climbed the literal mountain. He still works way too many hours, but it's what keeps him going. He's got the drive, passion, energy, and enthusiasm to make it all work. He doesn't want to let those people who are counting on him down—ever. Plus, when he gets up at 3:00 a.m. and gets to the stone yard, and he sees his name in lights, he can only smile proudly as he knows that's his name, and his name isn't on a rap sheet, an intake form, or a hospital bracelet. Don't take his success to mean he's gone soft. I'd think twice before trying to stiff him or make him look bad because this man knows how to box, and you don't want to be on the receiving end of that right cross!!

The Mitts story is really just beginning, and I'm proud to see him get shit done each and every day. In fact, that guy gets more shit done by the time he wakes up than most of us do in an entire day.

This is what he does.

CHAPTER THIRTEEN

Planting Seeds

Never stop working and never stop selling yourself. It doesn't matter where you are or what you are doing, the brand of YOU never stops. Letting people know who you are, what you do, and why you do it is important. Determine your brand and polish it. Then stick to it and own it. Think about the people in your life who dress a certain way or act in a certain manner. When you are out in the world, you are displaying your brand. Wear it loud and say it proud.

On four separate occasions, I've started my own business. While I've never considered myself to be an entrepreneur, I guess I must be entrepreneurial at the very least. I also am a grinder and subscribe to the theory that when opportunity isn't knocking, it's time to build a door.

Even when the door is built, you have to put forth incredible effort to ensure that folks know there is a door and where to find the knocker. So many people struggle with that aspect of telling their story. They are either too nervous to talk about themselves or their inner introvert comes out and they fear annoying people or the simple fear of rejection takes hold.

Starting a business and putting yourself out there is a challenge. Marketing, self-promotion, public relations, or any other form of attention-grabbing calls to action can be seen in a couple of different ways. Haters will always see you as a self-promoter. Supporters will see you as a hustler. Ignore the haters or turn them into supporters, but don't let them get in your way—ever.

I know many people who author opinion pieces, purchase display ads, appear on television as subject matter experts, or use social media to help promote their personal brand. All are terrific ways of letting the world know who you are and what you do. But you have to get hyper-focused on who your audience is and what you want your audience to see, hear, and ultimately act upon.

What I refer to as planting seeds includes all of the many tactics you will employ to fulfill your strategic goal(s). Who will you talk to? Who will you meet with? How will you reach them and how often? This all becomes critical in your outreach and, more importantly, in your follow-up. This is what separates the adults from the children. As I said in the beginning, follow-up is the king. People will do business with other people they know, like, and trust. One of the best ways of earning trust is by doing what you say. You have a meeting with a person on Monday, and you talk about that person's service business. In your follow-up email, what I've always tried to do is hit a few different things:

Speed—people like to be thanked, so do it quickly. I still strongly believe in the art of the handwritten note, because snail mail is called snail mail for a reason. The only living creature the tortoise might have been favored with in the race would have been the snail!! You can pick and choose your moments, but speed is imperative. In my meetings, I utilize technology and will draft a thank you from my car or the lobby of the office building—wherever makes the most sense. I want the thank you in the person's email inbox within ten minutes if possible.

Oftentimes, I might pre-draft the email "thank you" and have it sitting in my draft file. After the meeting, I will edit it appropriately if things went differently than anticipated or if I learned a new important fact.

Always reference something you learned—this could be a personal piece of information about the person or something important or relevant about the organization. Make sure to include this so the recipient knows you were listening.

Indicate some next step—let the person know you expect to hear from them by a specific date or that you will be contacting them and when.

FYI—if there is some story, article, or news item you think the person may be interested in, include it. I do this as a P.S. "I read this article and thought you may be interested as it really focuses on our discussion from today." What is it, and why are you sharing it? Just make sure it is a legitimate story from a solid resource and not some fake news you found on Facebook.

This is all so simple—so easy, yet so often overlooked. Countless times, I have acquiesced and agreed to a meeting or a sales call or an informational interview and didn't receive a thank you note. To make matters even more frustrating, when I am the interviewee, I always give some sort of follow-up. Call this person, read this article, or something. Those are my little tests to see how good you are at follow-up. If I take my time to sit down and meet with you (in person, Zoom, or on the phone), and you don't follow up with even a simple thank you, there is a pretty solid chance we won't be meeting again.

Then down the line, try to evaluate the opportunity to send a handwritten note. If you know the person's birthday, a card is always a nice gesture. In today's super-fast and high-tech world, it is incredibly noticeable when you open your mailbox and there is a handwritten envelope with a handwritten note inside. This goes farther than you will ever realize.

In addition to thank you notes and cards, what else can we do to stand out and make a difference? The most obvious to me is to stay true to your follow-up. If you say you are going to do something—anything—do it. If you say you will send a proposal by a certain date, send it hours earlier. If you have to submit a quote, send it early. A question was posed to you, and you owe an answer by a certain date—don't be late and don't forget. Your turn to schedule a breakfast or lunch—make sure it gets arranged. Be a person of your word and a person of high integrity. Remember—people do business with others who they know, like, and trust. Trust is earned, and for some, it can take months or even years to reach that point. Then, once you earn it, continue to earn it. Don't rest on your laurels under the presumption that you have the business and you don't need to work as hard.

A great sports analogy is that of Kobe Bryant. Kobe was arguably one of the five or six greatest basketball players of all time. His accomplishments are legendary, and his legacy will last several lifetimes. He was known as an eighth-grader and truly never disappointed. He went from high school state champion at Lower Merion to NBA champion with the Los Angeles Lakers. He was a fierce competitor and never stopped working. Kobe walked into practice every day as the best player on the court. That was not in dispute. However, he set the tone every day and at every practice by being the first to arrive, the last to depart, and the hardest-working member of his squad. This wasn't solely at the beginning of the season or the postseason. This was every day, every practice, all season long.

Kobe learned at an early age that good practice makes good players. Great practice makes great players. Kobe was determined to be the best. The season after he won his first NBA title, he began working out for the next season almost immediately. Time off would come when he was retired. The last five letters of the word R-E-T-I-R-E-D spell T-I-R-E-D, and Kobe never got tired. He fed off those who were tired at the end of the game and the end of the season. He outworked everyone, and it's possible that even with just a little less practice, he'd have still been the best.

But he left none of this to chance or speculation. He was going to make sure everyone knew how hard he worked. He did so in the hopes of making his coaches and teammates just a little bit better.

Since basketball is a team sport, with the whole being greater than the sum of its parts, hard work was going to be crucial.

The same is true in the workplace. You need to outwork, outhustle, and outmaneuver your competition. Get to every event, and get there early so you can see who is coming in and make early contact. Stay longer and meet late arrivers. Wake up early to attack email and follow up from the night before. Get started on attacking your own to-do list. There is never "nothing to do." Even if you are reading an article by a professional in your field, always be looking forward toward ways of being better, smarter, stronger, and faster. This is your professional livelihood. It is the difference between making good money and making great money. It could be the difference between working and being unemployed. You make your own luck, but never let anyone outwork or out-hustle you.

Because you have been attending events, using your social platforms for business, and developing a good CRM system, you now probably have built up a good list of contacts. Now you have to work that list. Who do you call, text, and reach out to meet in person? Some are a combination of all of the above, and it is up to you to determine the best course of communication. In addition to traditional forms of communication, if you can set yourself up as a subject matter expert, you should do so. A subject matter expert is someone who is relied upon by the press—local, regional, and national—for talking points and sound bites on topics in the news. Stories that will appear in the media need talking heads that understand the issues. Not everyone can be a subject matter expert due to the industry or their position within an organization. And, being on the local news is not the only way to get noticed.

Here are some differentiators on becoming a subject matter expert:

Share articles, stories, and opinion pieces from reputable news sources on your personal social media. Make sure your company allows you to post and represent yourself as someone working for the organization. If you read trade publications or industry journals or are just someone who is a news gatherer and collects information, share it widely. Make sure you properly credit the source, and tag as many relevant people as possible for potential larger distribution and readership. As an example, if you are in the waste removal business, and you see a great piece on sustainability and how it relates to corporate social responsibility, you should know that it may make for interesting reading for your friends and followers. Draft a simple one- or two-sentence introduction and then post the link to the story. You will be amazed at how many people haven't seen this story and will comment, like, and even re-share your post, exposing you and your organization to other people outside your immediate network.

Create original content using your social networks. A few of the social channels allow you the ability to write, edit, and post your own original thoughts in blog format. If you happen to have your own personal website, blog from there and then share your thoughts in a post with a link to your content. Again, add a simple introduction for readers to contextualize what they are reading.

Social media democratized content creation and sharing. In today's world, the media lines are blurred. Years ago, there were only a few news sources, and you had only so many alternatives to get your message across. With websites and social media, you can easily share your opinions, thoughts, and expertise with other people from across the world in seconds. This territory comes with great power and great risk. Written and shared words can help build your credibility but can also help tear you down. If you don't proofread your work or share inappropriate dialogue (and in today's world, the line between appropriate and inappropriate seems to change more often than some people change their socks), you will find yourself in more trouble. Take the old adage of measure twice and cut once and apply it to your work—proofread twice and hit send once!

Write a piece for your high school paper. As a graduate, your high school paper may be a great point to help you get noticed. Sure, the audience may not be filled with customers, but it gives you practice writing and begins to help you develop an audience and followers. After all, high school students quickly become college students and then (in theory) members of the workforce. I'm not suggesting you begin fishing for customers in high school, but you can begin to build credibility and develop your writing skills. For a high school paper, you could write about preparing for college, military experience, or the workforce—depending upon which route you choose. Or you could talk about a gap year, studying abroad, or the differences between two-year and four-year colleges.

The point is to consider your audience and think about the content you are preparing. However, the more practice you get (Kobe), the better you get, and the easier it will be to craft something later on when it is for a more established and professional audience.

You can do the same thing with your collegiate paper, fraternal organization newsletter, or any other affiliated entity with which you have been associated that has a written communication method for members.

Write for a very local weekly paper. Walk into any supermarket, and you will see local papers being given away. Usually, these periodicals are focused on hyper-local news from a municipality, but you may live in that area or be from that area, and you might have an interesting story or experience to share. Since most media have cut budgets and staff, any type of solid contributing piece of journalism might be appreciated. Read through some of the local papers (or online) and get a sense of the flavor and style of what they cover. Draft something that you believe will work with the cadence of what they present and then send an introductory email to the managing editor and share your piece, who you are, and what your connection is. You will be pleasantly surprised at the results.

Seek out small business and local podcasts. This year alone, there are over two million listed podcasts. Buy some recording equipment, and you too can have a podcast. If you don't want or need your own, you want to be a contributor on another. These small podcasters are searching for angles, looking for experts willing to tell their story. They seek fun, interesting, and reasonably dynamic personalities to tell their tales about business. If you are an introvert, this is a fantastic way to get your name out there. Podcasts are a conversation between you and the host. There isn't even a live audience. The conversation gets recorded, edited, and then posted and shared. By the time this happens, you will be long out of the studio and can listen along with everyone else. The fear of being an introvert and being judged immediately goes away.

Find local access cable television talk shows seeking guests with certain expertise. This will work like the podcast, but there will be cameras involved, so what you wear, how you sit, and what you look like all become important—as opposed to a podcast where you can wear whatever you want, and posture is less important. However, like Kobe, a good rule is to always be on your A-game…so dress the part and look the part when you are representing yourself and your organization.

Lastly, if you are someone who has the ability to be a subject matter expert in someone else's story—go for it. You really need to verify with your organization that appearing in the media to talk about your industry is copasetic with the employee handbook. Larger organizations have spokespeople designated as the only people who can speak to the media. This is to maintain the brand and the organizational talking points. When rogue individuals start talking to the media, especially those untrained in doing so, disaster can occur.

So learn the policy, and if you are able to speak to the press, make sure you are prepared. If it is television, make sure you have the right background; if it is radio, make sure you are in a quiet location with no distractions; and if it's print, really, the same rules apply. Try to get a sense of what you are going to speak about and what questions may come up so you can be prepared. Answer the questions succinctly and get the important points across early and often. Be authoritative and sound like an expert!!

Once you do this, more and more requests will come your way. And remember, if some is good, more is better. Begin to seek out these opportunities, and make sure you have a good place to serve as an aggregator for your personal media so that when you share one post, the link can possibly take readers to a library of additional resources where they can see you speaking or read your writing.

Now, once you have a new media to share, go back to the earlier part of this chapter and share, post, and be sure to tag the appropriate media partner. In all likelihood, the media company will re-share your post, and before you know it, your circle has increased. This is the best way to gain new followers and ultimately, more customers. That is the name of the game: How can you use your expertise to plant the seeds that help grow the biggest trees bearing the most fruit? Unless you are in the game just for fun, you are doing this to advance and enhance your career. That is always your goal—advance and enhance. Keep thinking about that and be focused. The prize is a better year every year.

The last piece of the puzzle of planting seeds is to simply remember to never quit. You are always on, always thinking about how to move forward, and always looking for who to meet, who to follow up with, and what your angle could be. You see a contact on the street, and you have a quick stop and chat. Get back to your computer and write a note to say how great it was to run into them and how you should make time for coffee or a meal.

Log everyone you know in your contacts and input as much data as you have on them, including birthday, anniversary, spouse or significant other's name, and anything else you can muster up. I have mastered the early happy birthday wish. Beginning at 5:00 p.m. on the prior day, I text or email (depending upon the relationship) the following message: Insert name—HBD—have a great day tomorrow and a better year ahead—all the best—Steve). I'm always the first to wish them a happy birthday, and it always gets noticed.

My rules about wishing someone a happy birthday are simple. If it is your really good friend and, in your circle, you text early and call the next day—actually pick up the phone and push the numbers to make a phone call. If voicemail picks up, leave an actual message!! If the person is a really good acquaintance, the early text is fine. You can add to that a social media wish too. If you just casually know the person, it's up to you. If the person is in my contacts, I text or email them. Social media wishes are for strangers and people you casually know. If your best friend is wishing you a happy birthday on social media and posting pictures but not calling you, that should be changed!!

But reach out and give someone an early happy birthday or anniversary. Recognize a great moment in their history. When I have a staff of employees, I always know what their anniversary date of hire is, and I do the same thing:

Dear_____,

Seven years ago, you started your career here, and I thank you for your time and effort and the energy you put in to make us a better organization each and every day. Have a great day and a better year ahead. All the best.

People want to be called out and recognized.

Plant seeds—they will grow. Before you know it, there will be a forest of all types of plants behind you. Some will bear fruit, others will keep you dry in the rain, and some will keep the sun from beating down on you. But each will serve a purpose. Figure out what tree came from what seed and what its best and highest value is. Then maximize it to the best of your ability.

CHAPTER FOURTEEN

Keeping the Faith

We have talked about the underdogs, but what about those times in life where success comes early and you seem destined for greatness? What happens if that greatness gets sidetracked? Do you give up and hide or do you reinvent yourself until you are back on the track of greatness?

So many young boys dream of playing sports at the highest possible level. We've discussed this already, but it is worth repeating. Everyone has dreams; they are what keep us motivated and, hopefully, focused. To play any sport at the highest level takes so many great character traits, and we have discussed them all. Hard work, determination, focus, and the ability to pick yourself up are all so important. The highest level of participation is different for everyone. What I say to everyone is, "The uniform comes off for everyone at some point…. For most kids, it's at the age of 12, and for extraordinary people like Tom Brady—it's 45." But one trait that often is overlooked is faith. What role does faith have in anything we do in life? How far can faith take us?

For as long as I can remember, I've followed the career of Tamir Goodman. Tamir was one of those young boys who fell in love with a game—basketball—and was intent on becoming the absolute best player, period. He had two older brothers whom he would follow to the gym to get shots up, rebound, and just hang around to learn the game.

Tamir's love for the game exploded, and he actually became a very good player. He was also fortunate to have an incredible support system in place, allowing him to not only follow his dream but to also do so with love—perhaps the greatest need people have. Tamir had an unquenchable thirst and an insatiable appetite for all things basketball related. Over time, he developed into one of the top players in the state of Maryland. He could shoot, handle, and pass and he played defense. He really always presented as a superstar in the making.

However, there was one thing that was very different about Tamir—he was (and is) an observant Orthodox Jew. He would not sacrifice his religious beliefs and participate in games or practices during the Jewish observance of Shabbat—Friday sundown through Saturday sundown every week or every year...ever.

You may recall stories about professional athletes like Sandy Koufax, one of the all-time great baseball players who played for the Los Angeles Dodgers. Sandy was a Jew. He wasn't Orthodox, but he was a proud Jew who refused to pitch in Game 1 of the 1965 World Series against Minnesota because it fell on Yom Kippur. Sandy was steadfast in his belief, and this was made easier because Dodgers manager Walter Alston supported Sandy, saying, "I can't let the boy do that to himself." While both Koufax and Alston hoped and prayed for rain, rain didn't come, and Sandy missed the game. (No worries; he pitched shutouts in Games 5 and 7).

Fast-forward to the late 1990s. Tamir was developing an incredible game and was a well-known name. So well known, in fact, that *Sports Illustrated* did a feature story on him, dubbing him "The Jewish Jordan." The name was, of course, in reference to Michael Jordan, and at that time, this was the greatest compliment a basketball player could receive. In 1999, when the article appeared, *Sports Illustrated* was one of the most important weekly magazines there was. Subscriptions were significant, and a cover story (minus a well-talked-about jinx) or a feature story was like gold. This was pre-social media, and Tamir blew up, to use today's terminology. Here was an Orthodox Jew who was playing basketball at an incredibly high level and had a major story focused on him in *Sports Illustrated*.

At the time, Tamir had also accomplished one of his lifelong dreams—he had accepted a scholarship to play basketball at the University of Maryland under Coach Gary Williams. Tamir was recruited by one of the all-time great collegiate basketball recruiters, Billy Hahn. Together, Williams and Hahn would ultimately lead Maryland to its only NCAA men's national championship in basketball—winning the coveted March Madness tournament in 2002.

Now here sat Tamir with a scholarship to Maryland, a *Sports Illustrated* feature story, and an entire career to be incredibly excited about. As a young boy, he knew he wanted to play Division I basketball, and he was not going to let his religious observances stand in the way. As a Maryland alum myself, I was so proud of the university for giving a scholarship to someone who was not only so talented but who was also a great ambassador for young Jewish boys looking to go as far as Tamir.

However, once it became abundantly clear that Tamir was really not going to play, practice, or be involved in formal team activities in any way on Shabbot, Maryland realized it had an issue. Eventually the university and Tamir parted ways, and the scholarship Tamir dreamed of was gone—because he wouldn't play basketball and turn his back on his faith at the same time. But he continued to work and he kept his faith.

Remember that Tamir was a hard and focused worker. Perhaps he got his drive from his *safta*, his grandmother, who lived in Israel much of the year and was a Holocaust survivor. For those of you who don't know much about the Holocaust, I urge you to learn and understand what it was like during the greatest tragedy in the history of mankind. However, if you have ever met a Holocaust survivor, you know these people are more than tough. What they lived through and can recall to help us ensure history does not repeat itself is absolutely incredible.

I have been fortunate to be able to spend time with many survivors. They inspire me more than they know, and I will always do whatever it takes to help them tell their story so that the world never forgets and this will never happen again.

So having a survivor so close to Tamir played a significant role in his determination and his faith. If his *safta* could not only survive but thrive after the Holocaust and be such an inspiration to Tamir, he had no choice but to keep fighting for what he wanted out of his basketball career.

Eventually a second Division I school approached Tamir. Towson University knew of Tamir and his situation. They also knew that having a player as special as Tamir far outweighed him not playing on Shabbat. So Tamir took his talents to Towson University. Not only did Tamir get to play Division I hoops, he was also the first freshman to start at Townson University in more than a decade. He had a solid freshman year, and then, unfortunate adversity struck in his sophomore year.

He ultimately did not finish his career at Towson University but instead was able to fulfill a second lifelong dream of playing professionally in Israel. If you don't know, professional basketball in Israel is top-notch. In my opinion, it is the second-best professional league in the world, and it attracts players from all over to participate. Tamir was recruited to play for the legendary Maccabi Tel Aviv team, coached by David Blatt. At that time, the world didn't know Coach Blatt, who ultimately would coach LeBron James and the Cleveland Cavaliers. What an incredible ride for Tamir and his family—he kept the faith, and the family never lost faith in him. Again, hard work and perseverance were important, but his faith was crucial.

After his first successful year playing professionally in Israel, Tamir joined the IDF. Israel has mandatory service when men and women hit a certain age. A country this small must maintain a well-trained army. Israel has among the finest in the world. Serving in the military in Israel is an honor. Young people grow up seeking to do so, and in fact, military service comes before college. If you are going to make a life in Israel, your peers won't ask you what college you went to; they will ask you what division you served and for how long.

Tamir was now a full-fledged Israeli and was truly living the dream he had for himself. Upon his arrival to Israel, one of the first people who reached out to him was Tal Brody—known as Mr. Basketball in Israel and perhaps the most well-known Israeli athlete of all time. Tal was born in New Jersey, and after being drafted into the NBA, he opted to become an Israeli citizen and play for the national basketball team. These kinds of relationships and contacts are common for Tamir. He learned early that a good-quality network is critical in helping to achieve any goal you have in life.

Unfortunately, Tamir's time on the basketball court over the next several years was wrought with injury. He suffered not one, not two, but three career-threatening injuries, and he fought through rehab and made it back after each one. However, as a high-level athlete, sustaining these types of injuries eventually took their toll. He even rehabbed while serving as an IDF soldier. This is a committed person who not only appreciates all the opportunities afforded him in life but also understands and relishes the responsibility that comes with all of it. It would have been easy to quit and do something else, but he wasn't built that way, and he certainly didn't learn about quitting from his *safta*, the Holocaust survivor. No, Tamir knew only one way forward, and yet again, his faith drove him to be the greatest he could be.

Eventually Tamir came to the realization that his playing days would come to an end. However, he was not finished with basketball. From a playing perspective, Tamir accomplished what was once seen as impossible. An observant Orthodox Jew who would not play or practice for a 24-hour period each week because of Shabbat and who wore a traditional Jewish head covering—the kippah—on his head played Division I basketball in the United States. He was recognized as being one of the great players, and he never backed down from an opponent—whether that opponent was on the court or that opponent was an injury or another distraction. Tamir met every challenge head-on and accomplished what so many wished they had.

But now, with his career over, how was he going to remain in the game and turn around and give back as both an entrepreneur and an Orthodox Jewish basketball star? His answer was easy—he developed a game simulator to help players improve their skills. Zone 190, as it was called, was used all the way up to and including the NCAA Women's Final Four. In 2007, Tamir realized that he wanted to give back to young people too. He started his now internationally recognized basketball camp, which has hosted thousands of children seeking to become both better basketball players and better humans.

Tamir's following in Israel and the United States, as well as his exceptional networking and people skills, have landed him some of the greatest players to ever play the game as guests of his in Israel and at his camps. Just this past summer—2022—Tamir hosted Auburn University and Coach Bruce Pearl for a series of exhibition games and camps. The young basketball-playing people of Israel are incredibly fortunate to have someone like Tamir working so hard on their behalf.

Of course, like everyone else, Tamir suffered a great setback during the COVID-19 pandemic. Camps were shuttered, and people were worried about transmission even through passing a basketball from one teammate to another. So what did Tamir do? He created another invention, and this one might be his best and most successful to date. The AVIV Net. This antimicrobial and moisture-wicking net dries the ball every time it passes through the basket. In addition, these basketball nets can be tailored to include a team or sponsor logo to help with branding. When you think about it, why wouldn't a team, facility, or university use these nets?

It doesn't hurt the on-field performance, and it provides an added layer of health and protection.

Tamir doesn't stop—he uses his contacts and his vast network to improve his own life and, thereby, the lives of others. He does not exist on this planet to help himself. He has successfully used his platform to increase opportunities for so many. He learned long ago that a great network is crucial to success. He also learned that doing what you say and living an honest and respectful life are so important.

Tamir is fortunate to have been blessed with a great combination of amazing talent and an incredible support system. He told me that he works so hard because G-d invests in each of us daily, and we have a responsibility to live the best life possible. We all have our own unique skill sets, and while we may not know immediately what those skills are, it is up to each of us to determine what they are and then ask ourselves: "Did we win the day?" Did we do all that we could and should have to be successful? If we were supposed to drive our kids to camp and pick them up, were we on time and did we follow the rules? Whatever it is you are meant to do, do it with all the eagerness you can.

Perhaps the most important piece to Tamir's life was his wife. They are blessed with five children who are learning incredible lessons from their parents. He is raising his children to be attracted to truth and to the values they believe in and can be inspired by. The Goodmans emphasize what is important—respect, safety, sharing, giving, and, of course, faith. If you can truly understand these important values and incorporate them into your life each day, you will not only learn to get shit done, but you will also do so in a way that is so meaningful.

Will you play Division I college hoops and then play professionally overseas? Who knows. Everyone is built to a certain capacity, but not everyone fills their own cup. The common theme of this book up until now has been hard work, determination, perseverance, honesty, and a mix of a little bit of luck and good timing. I thought those were the key ingredients. After spending time with Tamir and watching his career over all of these years, I realized adding faith to this mix is really important.

So go out and win the day but do so in the best way possible. And if things aren't going your way, remember to keep the faith.

CHAPTER FIFTEEN

The Tribe Has Spoken

What you is going to show up when? If you are always on brand, YOU will always be YOU. If you are different people depending upon the situation, then you will have trouble ahead. Don't get voted off of the island because people have trouble understanding who the real you is. It's okay if not everyone likes you—that's normal. But be your best self.

Twenty-one years ago, prime-time television changed forever. A show called *Survivor* debuted on CBS and has had an incredible run of great ratings for more than two decades. The premise of the show is to be the last person standing without having been "voted off of the island." It is billed as the greatest social experiment in society, as it brings together approximately 18 strangers on an island with only the clothes on their backs who must "outwit, outlast, and outplay" the others through many of the ideas and values we have discussed so far. Networking, contacts, follow-up, and getting shit done are the secrets to success. Participants must make friends, create allies, determine who their competition is, and attempt to vote those people off before they get voted off.

The difference is *Survivor* is a game and not real life, but it is a game played for one million dollars. It also gives players the opportunity to recreate and reinvent their personas and either create a new way to present themselves or double down on their same character flaws. These flaws are hard for others to deal with in the real world—they are even more exposed when you are half-naked running around an island barely eating 300 calories a day.

What this show and this game do force you to do as a participant and notice as a viewer is the art of persuasion and human interaction. It's a game where the strong, smart, and beautiful don't always succeed. The stronger you present, the better chance you have to get taken out. In the real world, it is very different. Oftentimes, it is the biggest, strongest, fastest, smartest, and loveliest who get the promotion, the raise, the call up to the next level, or seemingly advance. Is *Survivor* the retribution of the little people, or is it simply people realizing their network really is critical and who they ally themselves with matters the most? I don't know the answer, but I have never missed an episode of this show because it truly is an incredible look into how people approach human interaction. How will they build their network when all they have are the clothes on their backs? How will they act and react to situations in which they are both uncomfortable and unfamiliar?

Think about *Survivor* in the real world. How do you react in the same types of situations? Imagine if your job were set on an island and you had to compete for a promotion. You are a director at your organization, and you are hoping to be promoted to vice president. There is only one vice president role, but there are 16 directors vying for the opportunity to be named as the newest member of the executive team. But instead of your boss relying solely on the resume you've built while working at the organization, you were told to get on a plane and fly to a remote island with the other directors. The last person left standing would become the new vice president.

Now you get to the island, and there you are in your skimpiest attire, preparing to compete in contests of mental capacity and physical strength. You will then be taken to a group meeting where the person with the most votes is eliminated and your chances to become vice president increase. You have to immediately assess your situation and determine who you want to be aligned with, who your biggest threats are, and who should be eliminated and in what order. If you see yourself as a target, maybe you want to keep bigger targets around longer. If you are someone who is seen as a long shot for promotion, maybe it doesn't matter. The point is, relationships, alliances, friendships, and confidants are crucial, regardless of whether you are on an island or in the real world seeking to get ahead.

Your network is crucial. Having the right people in your contacts is something you must develop and continuously work on from the time you get out into the workplace. People you meet early in your career could become your boss or co-worker. They could become vendors or clients. Whoever and wherever these people cross paths with you again, you don't want them to "vote you off the island." You want them to see you and remember you as an ally. Someone who they liked as a person or valued in some manner. Most importantly, you are someone they trust and know they can continue to trust in a professional setting. This is how you build your network, and ultimately, what I refer to as your advisory council. Who you talk to about what. More importantly, when you talk to them and how.

The common theme I've been trying to give to you is the importance of networking. In life, we have two options—we can either lower the river or raise the bridge. By lowering the river, we rid ourselves of all unnecessary people, places, and things. We cut the noise and the distractions and try to eliminate much of the negativity that surrounds us. Once we lower the river, and we feel we are at a place where we can begin to thrive, we must focus on raising the bridge.

In order to raise the bridge, we go out and find mentors and contacts who can help us. We continue on as lifelong learners, trying to better educate ourselves in both traditional and non-traditional ways. Not everyone can or will have a college education. Fewer will have post-graduate degrees. However, you can always learn new things, teach yourself new tricks, and gain a better education. By doing so, you are elevating your personal growth, which ultimately increases your brand.

Who are going to be your allies? Your consiglieres? Your go-to people? According to a variety of sources, including *Psychology Today*, the average person makes close to 35,000 decisions per day. Think about that—35,000 decisions!! How many did you just make? More than you realize. With this many decisions in front of you, you need assistance. This isn't a game show, and you don't get to phone a friend or use a lifeline. You show up and are presented with questions needing answers. We make decisions we don't even realize we are making, but 35,000 is a lot of thinking and even more doing. Clearly, most of these decisions are very simple and need little to no discussion. However, we are often faced with much more important and critical paths we must choose from—do we zig or zag? This is when our networks are crucial as we never know who we will need to call upon or when.

I cannot stress enough that networks need a lot of work. Meeting someone one time does not automatically put that person in your network. Constant follow-up, meetings, and multiple touch points put them into your sphere of influence. That is what you are seeking. Some people will always just be casual acquaintances whom you call upon for arm's length transactions. Others will be much more rooted in your decision tree.

Think about your time on the island. How will you make your contacts? Always consider yourself armed with nothing but the clothes on your back. Pretend the world is watching and critiquing your every thought and move. Who will you choose to move forward with, and how will those choices help or hurt you? Sometimes, you have little to no time to make choices, so you have to rely on your gut. Your gut comes from your past experiences. Most people remind you of someone, so try to quickly identify their social doppelganger and choose wisely. The good news is, these aren't life or death decisions—at least on the surface. But you want to expand your network and make it the best it can possibly be. At the end of the day, you never want to hear, "The tribe has spoken," and your time has ended on the island. Try to be the last person standing.

CHAPTER SIXTEEN

Can I Pick Your Brain? (Curiosity Killed the Cat, but It Won't Kill You)

Going from mentee to mentor is not easy. What do you do when you achieve some success? Society will measure you in a lot of ways, but giving back and paying it forward is one of them. This is also a great way to expand your network with a new set of people. Remember that everyone you meet—younger or older—is part of your network.

As a young person, I did everything I could to reach out and meet with more accomplished people. At that time in my life, pretty much everyone was more accomplished than me. I was still working for the Washington Bullets, running around, doing whatever I was told to do, and still paying for my fake phone call sins, but I knew the Bullets were not going to be my forever stop. On one hand, I woke up every day grateful and thankful for the opportunity to work for a team in the National Basketball Association as I was truly fulfilling my dream of a sports business career. I knew the road would be long and paved with bumps and ditches, but I was not willing to hit those ditches in the Washington, DC metro area.

I was finishing school at the same time at the University of Maryland, taking classes at night and on weekends and doing everything possible to finish on time. I was paying my own way through college, and I didn't have any money for additional schooling. In addition to my time working for the Bullets and going to school, I was also selling women's shoes at Bakers. The district manager at the parent company—Edison Brothers—was constantly asking me to become a full-time manager with the possibility of quickly growing into a district manager. I was toiling for a small salary, but the opportunity was great, but I saw my future in the league office in New York. The skills I learned selling shoes were invaluable, and I probably could have made a decent living in that business, but I was not willing to give up my dream at such a young age.

So in addition to everything else I was doing, I began reaching out to people for informational interviews and meetings. The goal was to get my name out there, and with every meeting, try to get an additional name or two to meet with. It was actually in-person LinkedIn. Had I realized what I was doing and could have had some vision, maybe I'd have come up with a platform like LinkedIn…but as the saying goes, "If the queen had balls, she'd be the king." By the way, I know I just offended, like, 100 people with that remark, but it's just a saying!! Anyway, I would go out and meet with anyone in sports who was willing to meet with me. I was taking the train to New York City and Philadelphia or getting on calls with people in other cities. And that is when you had to pay long-distance charges!!

For the most part, people were willing to meet with and talk to me. I learned early on that the trick for success was to ask them questions about themselves and get them talking about the work they did and how they got where they were. To me, they were very important and accomplished people. I knew early not to make the meeting about me and my wishes, hopes, and dreams. People love to talk about themselves and tell you their stories.

What I didn't know then but I know now is, the question "Can I pick your brain?" is very intimidating to people. People are busy and don't want to waste their time on young people who aren't serious. As someone who is now on the other side of that question, it is one of those situations where you just go, "Ugh." Depending on who the requester of your time is, you probably can't say no. Today, more and more of that exists. What makes it worse today is that it is oftentimes a parent, grandparent, guardian, or some other adult asking, "Hey, will you do me a favor and talk to my son/daughter about their career and who they can talk to about finding a job?" This makes the favor ten times worse. Because now you don't really know if the young person is interested or if the adult is pushing. Or, is the young person incapable of making the request?

My typical response to an adult goes something like this: "I'd be more than happy to speak to your son/daughter. Have them reach out to me directly, and we will set something up." I'm not interested in having Mommy or Daddy play the middle role. If the younger person follows up with me, great—no problem. We will meet, talk, or get together in some fashion. The crazy part is that more than 50 percent of these requests go unfulfilled—meaning I tell the adult to have the younger person reach out, and in at least half of these situations I was never contacted. Talk about a colossal waste of my time.

In that rare instance when I do receive actual follow-up from the person seeking my advice or guidance, I follow a strict three-step process to continue to test their readiness and interest. First, I ask them to send me a cover note as if they didn't know me explaining why they want to meet, along with a resume or summary of qualifications depending upon where they are in their journey. After receiving these documents, I will follow up (usually within an hour) and ask them to follow up with me by phone on a certain day and within a certain timeframe. Asking for a specific time is not fair to them as I don't know what else they have going on. I do say that if they have any conflicts to let me know, and I will suggest alternative days or times. Lastly, after we speak, I wait for a timely thank you. We've already discussed what I see as timely. If I don't receive a thank you within a very reasonable amount of time (like, by the end of that day), I will more than likely lose almost all interest in this person.

Presuming someone meets all of these criteria, and I see they are serious, there is nothing I enjoy more than sitting down with young people interested in a career that I can possibly be helpful with. I will do one of four things to assist:

- Offer guidance in terms of career path suggestions and ideas
- Give them actual names and contact information on who to call and the ability to utilize my name as a reference
- Do a personal email introduction myself to a contact who I think can be helpful
- Offer to remain a resource in their career search

If you are someone who has been taught the importance of follow-up and listening, you and I will get along famously, and I will be a dogged advocate for you in your pursuit of the best job possible. I'd say, without question, I've been directly responsible for close to 600 people getting jobs over the past 30-plus years. The number goes higher if you count indirect suggestions and referrals. I do this all because it's the right thing to do and in the hopes that if I'm ever in need, someone might do the same for me. But really, helping people out—especially those coming up the ranks behind us—is one of the most important things we should be doing as the more-established generation. We want to ensure we are developing a highly productive and responsible working class who will remember there was someone there for them so they can pay it forward down the line.

There are people who do this for a living—recruiters, headhunters, placement specialists—who are all supposedly great at helping find people jobs. Perhaps in another life, I could have done this type of work. However, one of the things that makes me so successful is the fact that I do this in a genuine and authentic way. Both parties know I'm not prospering financially, and my interest in any connection I make is for the betterment of both the individual and the organization. Once you establish this level of respect and expertise, your word becomes so important. I've heard numerous times about how important a recommendation or referral from me is for both the organization and the candidate. As a neutral party, I'm perceived as someone who has both parties' best interests at heart.

So along the way you will be asked by others for your time. It can be a request that interrupts your day or week. Take it as an opportunity to give back and to expand your network. It won't happen right away, but if you think back to the chapter in this book on planting seeds—these are the ultimate seeds. I can look back now after more than three decades, and with 600-plus people in positions, my network has expanded. I can call each and every one of those people anytime and for any reason. They are real contacts who can and will be helpful to me as a resource in business. That could mean a referral or a lead generator or a connector. It may seem like work at the beginning, but do your best to help these people. Put the emphasis on the requesting party and see how their follow-up is but enjoy the journey of meeting a younger version of you. Remember what it was like as you were starting out and seeking advice and wisdom from those more established in the workforce.

You will be surprised at how much you might learn from them and how much the world is evolving in front of your eyes. I think back to when I was their age and the resources I had compared to what is now available. I've definitely come away learning a trick or two about technology and about things going on in pop culture. To me, it is critical to remain relevant, and one of the easiest and best ways to do so is to talk to and meet with younger people and learn their perspectives. What are they watching, reading, and listening to? Think about when you were younger and how the generations ahead of us had a harder time keeping up with what we were doing. Today's world is easier to catch up on; it's easier to learn what's hot. Stay relevant and interesting because your next boss, your next adventure, or your next anything could be or involve working with someone significantly younger than you.

George Bernard Shaw was famously quoted in the 1930s as saying, "Youth is wasted on the young." He meant that young people's lack of experience does not allow them to fully appreciate what it is they are experiencing at any given moment. The joy of great success may not feel as great and failure may seem even crueler. However, as you gain more experience in life, it is easier to value and understand what life is presenting you. Hence, part of our responsibility as more experienced, senior leaders is to impart our wisdom and experience to those coming up behind us—especially those who are actively and outwardly seeking our advice and counsel. But never stop being a lifelong learner, and try to come out of every conversation with some extra nugget of information. One more tidbit you can use to impress your friends, children, or co-workers. It will make the experience so much better. So the next time someone asks you if they can pick your brain or get some time on your calendar, say yes and pick their brain right back.

CHAPTER SEVENTEEN

Hey, You Look Familiar

Don't judge a book by its cover. People are not always what they appear or how they look. Everyone has a different and sometimes difficult story. We tend to judge people based on our stories, but that isn't fair. Everyone needs some help and many need a break. How will you respond to someone who looks and acts differently than you?

When I was in seventh grade, there was an eighth-grader named Frank Walls (not his real name). Frank was a terrific kid who always brought the fun. It was good that I got to know him because when I made it to eighth grade, there was an eighth-grader named Frank Walls. Same kid—didn't make it the first time so he had to do it all over again. We became pretty good buddies, and it was easy to see Frank was a pretty smart kid who just didn't really try. I think he cared, but who can ever know who really cares about anything?

This was all going to be really painful for Frank because when I was in ninth grade, there was still an eighth-grader named Frank Walls. Three years in eighth grade. This was before it took a village and when it was still okay to leave a child behind, I suppose. In school, there is a judgment system, and it never seemed unfair. You go to class, pay attention, receive assignments—either in class or as homework—complete the work, turn it in, take exams, and are graded based on both your participation in finishing the assigned work and on your proficiency with the tests. Seems like a reasonable system and not unlike what life might offer you. While you don't get graded in life, you do receive promotions, raises, and bonuses in work based on your ability to do not only what you are supposed to do but also on your ability to do it exceedingly well while demonstrating excellence in any and every way possible.

So in school if you don't do the work, don't prepare, and don't do well on a test, your instructor will know immediately and grade your results accordingly. Teachers don't enjoy giving bad grades. I spoke to several in preparing this chapter and every single person I spoke to said a bad grade is just as much a reflection on them as it is on the student. A teacher who can't motivate or get through to a student must be incredibly frustrated.

School is the first place for young people to learn how to meet others, make friends, navigate hard choices, and deal with difficult people. You don't realize you are learning these skills, but you are. In some instances, you may even be learning bad habits. However, in addition to classroom education, social skill development is perhaps the most important thing you will learn in those formative years.

One of the challenges young people face is how to interact in school. They say youth is wasted on the young. I never understood this saying until I got older. When we are kids, we can't wait for school to be over each day and each week, and our happiest day is the last day of school each year. The thought of summer school? NO WAY!!! Summer is for hanging out, having fun, going to camp, playing sports, and going on trips—wherever those trips may be. But school is a bummer. Homework, assignments, studying, exams, mean girls, mean boys, bullying, assemblies—you name it and we hated it. Except that we were wrong!! It was the greatest. What were we thinking?! We were with our friends all day. Our day ended in the middle of the afternoon and we had either sports or other assorted activities. There was no stress. Tests or homework? What wouldn't you trade to go back to do it all over again? That is one of the main points of "Youth is wasted on the young." We are so anxious for it to go by quickly, end as fast as possible. We want to grow up, get bigger, go into the real world, and make money. What were we thinking?!

What does the real world have to offer? When is spring break or winter break? Where are the teacher in-service days off? When can we leave early to catch the bus for our afternoon sports or activities? When do we get the summer off?! If I'm missing something, please let me know and tell me where to sign up.

If you're a student, understand your place in school and how to use it to better yourself. By that, I don't mean grow up too fast and not make time to be a kid. But learn how to interact with adults. How to budget your time so that you can study, have fun, and possibly even make time to have a part-time job. Set meetings up with teachers before or after school. Teachers want to work with students who make an effort. Show up to class, do your work, make an appointment or two, and be friendly. Acknowledge your teacher—say hello. Learn their birthday and wish HBD on their day. Just learn how to interact as a human being. I can assure you that Frank Walls would not have done three years of eighth grade had he followed this basic script.

This was back before the days of "Leave no child behind," as I stated earlier. Oftentimes people get left behind because they can't keep up and should be left behind. If you are running a 10k, and you train and prepare and are 100 percent ready when the starting gun goes off, you don't sit around and wait for those who just entered for fun to see if they can actually finish. No—you go as fast as you can and you finish. You do well before those stragglers who put in little to no effort, didn't prepare or train, and didn't take it seriously.

Everything doesn't have to be an even playing field. Some people study and do well in school and go on for post-graduate degrees or other advanced studies. Many of these people go on to become high achievers and high earners. Should we begrudge them the sacrifices they most likely made to get where they are? What about the people who don't work hard, don't finish school, and have lower-paying careers? You can't just arbitrarily lump people into categories and make judgments. But regardless—those who can move ahead should be applauded and should not have to sit around and wait for those who didn't work as hard.

These examples are plentiful and you can think of many in your own life. The point is, some people are going to be ahead and others behind. That is life. It's okay to leave people behind as everyone will eventually find their own way and their own place. The world is a meritocracy—eat what you kill—and you should all be thinking of ways to prepare yourself to be the best possible you. Don't try to be someone else. You can certainly take and emulate good qualities from people you admire and respect, but shape those characteristics into your own and become the best possible you that there is. That is really all the world expects. Nobody else can be you, and frankly, nobody else wants to be you.

CHAPTER EIGHTEEN

Hello, Neighbor

Don't be afraid to follow advice and listen to others. There are many great philosophers and leaders who speak to us differently than we speak to each other. The influential people speak in a way where we will want to re-quote them. Oftentimes their messaging is on point and inspiring. Others have little to say. Find those people you admire or are drawn to and read their works and listen to them often.

I love quotes, sayings, and analogies. I use them all the time and in all situations. Sometimes they are funny one-liners; sometimes I use them to make a point. I write a great deal and will refer to a quote to emphasize or summarize an issue, and sometimes I just enjoy referring to something that is really well-said.

My generation uses quotes in another form too. We quote great movie lines and have inserted those into our everyday jargon. Not a day goes by when I'm not saying something from a movie from my past to a family member, friend, or close associate. Again, these soften a mood, poke good fun at a moment, or can really sum up a story. Who doesn't play a round of golf without a good *Caddyshack* quote? You get the point.

One of my favorite people to quote when writing and speaking is Fred Rogers—yes, Mr. Rogers from the Neighborhood. I grew up during a time when there were only five television channels and the only one with children's programming other than Saturday mornings was the Public Broadcasting Service. So we watched *Mr.*

Rogers' Neighborhood, *Sesame Street*, *Zoom*, and *The Electric Company*. I swear I watched *Mr. Rogers* when I was in elementary school as there was nothing else to watch. Moreover, I literally grew up in Mr. Rogers' Neighborhood of Squirrel Hill. This national figure of good and decency. This man, who was single-handedly teaching children around the United States about good vs. evil and other important life lessons, lived just a few blocks from where I grew up. He was a mainstay of our community and someone we were incredibly proud to call our own.

One of my favorite Mr. Rogers quotes is one that I have used often in both speaking and writing. It has been particularly effective during the COVID-19 crisis and specifically during the beginning when people were scared and confused. I was leading an organization responsible for tens of thousands of people who were looking to us/ me for advice and leadership. We were conducting weekly briefings, daily updates, and as-necessary informational sessions.

Mr. Rogers said, "When I was a boy and I would see scary things in the news, my mother would say to me, look for the helpers. You will always find people who are helping." This was a quote I'd remembered from growing up. While I didn't have Fred Rogers's delivery or tone, I understood his message and was able to relay it to our community on several occasions. I felt that in the moment, and certainly to a specific demographic, Fred Rogers would resonate strongly with his messaging.

Mr. Rogers has many great quotes. While his main mission was to make the complex world simple for children, I have always believed he was smart enough to impact adults in a meaningful way. As an example, he said, "We speak with more than our mouths. We listen with more than our ears." Think about that quote the next time you are at an event or are just simply having a conversation with someone. Are you fully engaged? What are your nonverbal cues giving off? Are your eyes wandering, feet tapping, or are you looking at your phone? How do you feel when you are trying to talk to someone else and you know that person is not fully with you? That he/she is off thinking about someone else or where else they could be or where the bathroom is? It's frustrating. Be present with people. Make people feel like you are truly interested and they are really interesting. It goes a long way and it's the same type of respect you want when you are talking.

I could write 10,000 words on Fred Rogers alone. He was a great man who did great things in a great community. Squirrel Hill was, is, and always will be one of the all-time great neighborhoods. I was blessed to have grown up in a community with such real people who cared. The show *Cheers* famously had a line in the theme song: "where everybody knows your name…" That was Squirrel Hill. Parents and grandparents were never worried about letting kids run freely because there was always someone watching out. If you needed a drink or something to eat or a bathroom to use, you always had one. We knew the cops, the crossing guards, and the store owners. Everybody had a name and a story. These weren't good times; they were great times. It is where I learned everything I needed to learn. Mr. Rogers epitomized all that was good, not just in the world, but he was our guy. He let all of you into his neighborhood, but that neighborhood was ours.

There are so many other great quotes that I use often. Some of them are probably considered inappropriate in today's world, where everything you say offends somebody somewhere. We had a strict code growing up. "Sticks and stones may break my bones, but words will never hurt me." Sounds goofy but it stuck.

Some of the other people I quote from who are incredible leaders in history include Martin Luther King Jr. and Oprah Winfrey. If you look back at what Martin Luther King was able to accomplish and you focus on what he said and did, you will see that he was one of the kings of getting shit done. That man went where few men who looked like him dared to go or even dreamed of going. To me, there is no question the world would be a different place had he not been sadly murdered. He exuded what it meant to be a leader and he was a true visionary.

One of my favorite quotes from Martin Luther King, Jr. is: "Make a career of humanity. Commit yourself to the noble struggle for equal rights. You will make a better person of yourself, a greater nation of your country, and a finer world to live in." This is exactly where we all want to be. This entire book is about making yourself better. Understanding how to stand out in a world of people looking to stand out. What tricks you can use to grow your network and keep people engaged in your work. While it is all about you, it's important to make the world a better place.

As mentioned in an earlier chapter, the late, great comedian Rodney Dangerfield would say, "You have to look out for number one. Just don't step in number two." It is incumbent upon each of us to be great promoters of our work and our accomplishments. If we don't toot our own horns, who will? However, as we climb the corporate and social ladders we can and must reach back down to those less fortunate. We must pay it forward and leave the world a better place than we found it.

Remember that life is simpler if we mow and plow around the stump, but your yard will look a whole lot better if you go the extra mile and remove the stump. Hard work is hard for a reason. Shortcuts seldom get you anyplace faster—it only seems like they do. If you don't take the time to do something right, you better believe you are going to find the time to do something twice.

Walk with your head held high and do what's right. Find your mentor(s) and keep them in your inner circle. Remember that every path you choose will have a few puddles—some will be big and some will be small. Sometimes the puddles will be unavoidable, and your shoes will get wet. What you do next is what matters the most.

Try to use good judgment and make good decisions. Good judgment comes from experience, and most of that comes from bad judgment. It's okay to fail and make mistakes. That is part of our journey. Remember that you can't enjoy victory without realizing the taste of defeat. But take success in stride. Never forget where you came from and where you started. Some people start on third base, but most aren't even on the bench when the game begins. If you think you're important and wield a lot of influence, try ordering someone else's dog around and see how that works out.

Lastly, if you find yourself in a hole, the first thing to do is stop digging since it's most likely your actions and decisions that put you there. Take responsibility for your own actions. Others are not to blame for whatever mess we find ourselves in. This is exactly why we need a great network of smart, confident, rational, trustworthy, and caring people surrounding us wherever we are. In turn, we need to learn to be there for others as part of their network.

This is the world Fred Rogers imagined and hoped for. In his show, it was the land of make-believe. The world isn't perfect and neither are we—but we can have great and productive lives if we keep our heads up, work hard, and work smart.

Over the years, I've read and reread a number of books and I want to share the list with all of you. While these are in no particular order, there is a reason Dale Carnegie's book is at the top. I read this book every year. It is the number one best-selling business book of all time and if you haven't read it, you should. The rest of the list are books I've enjoyed. I try to take snippets of information from everything I read.

I've also included some go-to websites I have on my favorites list. It is human nature to continue to evolve. None of us have all the answers, so it's well worth taking the time to explore the resources below, as well as the information found in many other books and websites. Find the authors and titles that call to you. Hopefully my book will make someone else's recommended reading list someday.

Books

How to Win Friends and Influence People: The Only Book You Need to Lead You to Success
Dale Carnegie

Swim with the Sharks without Being Eaten Alive: Outmotivate, and Outnegotiate Your Competition
Harvey Mackay

From Strength to Strength: Finding Success, Happiness, and Deep Purpose in the Second Half of Life
Arthur C. Brooks

The Tipping Point: How Little Things Can Make a Big Difference
Malcolm Gladwell

The Power of Regret: How Looking Backward Moves Us Forward
Daniel H. Pink

The Prime Ministers: An Intimate Narrative of Israeli Leadership
Yehuda Avner

Wooden on Leadership: How to Create a Winning Organization
John Wooden and Steve Jamison

The Art of War
Sun Tzu

Leaders Eat Last: Why Some Teams Pull Together and Others Don't
Simon Sinek

Do Hard Things: Why We Get Resilience Wrong and the Surprising Science of Real Toughness
Steve Magness

Chip Wood Carry Water: How to Fall in Love with the Process of Becoming Great
Joshua Medcalf

Customer Centricity: Focus on the Right Customers for Strategic Advantage
Peter Fader

The Power of Positive Thinking
Norman Vincent Peale

Tuesdays With Morrie: An Old Man, a Young Man, and Life's Greatest Lesson
Mitch Albom

Reagan on Leadership: Executive Lessons from the Great Communicator
James Strock and Tom Peters

Freakonomics: A Rogue Economist Explores the Hidden Side of Everything
Steven D. Levitt and Stephen J. Dubner

The Logic of Sports Betting
Ed Miller and Matthew Davidow

Good Neighbor: The Life and Work of Fred Rogers
Maxwell King

Where Do We Go from Here: Chaos or Community?
Dr. Martin Luther King, Jr.

Call Him Jack: The Story of Jackie Robinson, Black Freedom Fighter
Yohuru Williams and Michael G. Long

It Worked for Me: In Life and Leadership
Colin Powell

Where Have All the Leaders Gone?
Lee Iacocca

The Way I Heard It
Mike Rowe

*When McKinsey Comes to Town: The Hidden Influence of the World's
Most Powerful Consulting Firm*
Walt Bogdanich and Michael Forsythe

Websites

https://leadershipfreak.blog/
https://www.theringer.com/
https://www.ted.com/
https://www.linkedin.com/
https://freebeacon.com/
https://www.sportsbusinessjournal.com/
https://www.wsj.com/
https://foxsportsradio.iheart.com/
https://www.si.com/
https://www.dalecarnegie.com/
https://fivethirtyeight.com/
https://thehill.com/
https://newrepublic.com/latest
https://www.vanityfair.com/
https://www.gq.com/
https://www.menshealth.com/
https://www.theatlantic.com/
https://www.aspeninstitute.org/
https://www.forbes.com/
https://www.psychologytoday.com/
https://theathletic.com/
https://variety.com/
https://greaterthanthegame.org/
https://www.fastcompany.com/
https://thetaclv.com/
https://www.sportico.com/author/johnwallstreet/

Acknowledgments

Writing a book takes incredible time, patience, and focus. I was able to find an inordinate amount of time that I didn't plan for early in 2022. I began drafting an outline for what this book could look like and I went for it. It's been an incredible journey—fun, interesting, exhilarating, and ultimately wonderfully satisfying.

My family has been an incredible source of pride and inspiration to me. I would not have been able to endeavor upon this important project without their support and love. My brother, Evan, whom I don't get to see nearly enough, has always been an inspiration to me. We've always been close as we really helped raise each other. He's an all-star and a super successful businessperson still living in our hometown. Watching him succeed in the manner he has has brought me great joy.

My wife, Lori, is a superstar. Most of the women at this point in our lives are enjoying full-time yoga, pickleball, tennis, or whatever it is they do. Not my wife—she runs a major law firm that she built and works seventy hours per week, every week. She is hyper-focused on being the best lawyer she can be, and if you ask her peers, she has accomplished her goal. She has been an almost perfect role model to young women all around and especially her daughter.

Samantha and Ethan, my two stepchildren, are like my own children. They've been in my life for a very long time, and while we don't share the same last name, we share an incredible bond and love. I'm at the top of their fan club and couldn't imagine life without them.

Jake and Sam—my two offspring who changed my life. Words can't express what it meant to me when I heard, "It's a boy" twice!! Both born at the same time of day four years apart, these two have been all the inspiration I could ever ask for. Everything I've ever done has been for them.

To all my friends, my real friends—thank you for your unwavering support and your dogged determination to keep me focused. The fellas from back home are more than friends—they are brothers from other mothers, but we've been friends since Colfax and will remain so forever.

My Philly guys whom I've known for a long time—you all are brothers in a different way.

I could thank so many more people, but you don't want to read all of my thanks. I'm the product of two incredible grandparents who gave up their golden years to raise my brother and me. My mom's parents, her sister, my dad's brother, and so many others were there to assist. I have so many memories of great aunts, uncles, and cousins.

So I hope you enjoy the stories and the little pieces of advice I've learned along the way. It's a big world out there—once you make it smaller, it's much easier to navigate. Just put yourself in a strong position and remember to always drink upstream from the herd.

About the Author

STEVE ROSENBERG has managed, marketed, and operated some of America's best-known and most interesting events, concepts, and projects—Celebrity All Star Hockey to the National Hockey League neutral site games, The Book and the Cook Fair, Welcome America Festival, Disney's World on Ice, Nickelodeon Live, the WWE, Ringling Bros. and Barnum & Bailey Circus, and many more. He has been part of the grand opening team of eight public assembly facilities across the U.S., including the Pepsi Center, WonderWorks, National Constitution Center, Independence Visitor Center, and Colorado's Ocean Journey.

He began his career with the Washington Bullets (now Wizards) where he learned how to manage multiple bosses and requests. He learned very quickly that the person who is able to get the most done in an efficient manner is going to go the farthest, and be the most productive. Throughout his career, he has been called upon to make things happen when others were unable to do so. When he hears "no," that is when his instincts take over. A serial networker and relationship builder, Rosenberg understands that a person's success is not only predicated upon the contacts they make. The follow-up and how those relationships build over time are equally important.

Rosenberg earned a degree in sports management from the University of Maryland. He is on the board of several civic and nonprofit organizations, including as a Co-Founder of Philadelphia Youth Basketball, City of Philadelphia Army Navy Game Host

Committee, the World Maccabiah Games, and the International Jewish Sports Hall of Fame, and he is Board Chair of the Philadelphia Jewish Sports Hall of Fame. He is also very involved in Coaches vs. Cancer, the Pete and Jameer Nelson Foundation, and the K-Low Elite AAU. He spends his free time volunteering with youth-based organizations. He has been an adjunct professor in the School of Tourism and Hospitality at Temple University.

Originally from Pittsburgh, Rosenberg lives in Center City Philadelphia with his wife, Lori.